Death of the Traditional Real Estate Agent:
Rise of the Super-Profitable Real Estate Sales Team

Death of the Traditional Real Estate Agent:
Rise of the Super-Profitable Real Estate Sales Team

by Craig Proctor and Todd Walters

To order additional copies of this book, contact:
Xlibris
1-888-795-4274
www.Xlibris.com
Orders@Xlibris.com
709493

Contents

Foreword

Death . . . is just a word. Or is it? For sure it's a powerful 'word'. In fact if you stop and think about it for a minute, 'words' can propel you to incredible levels of success selling real estate or they can leave you without any business to speak of.

Since I entered the real estate industry in 1990, I have seen a lot of changes. I remember when there was no MLS on computer, there was simply a book released each month with area real estate company's listings. I remember when there were no cell phones readily used by agents; no internet used by agents and absolutely no social media. I could go on and on and on about all of that. In doing so, I would bore, even confuse you, as to why we are writing this book, why it's relevant to you, important that you read it and study its words. So I will stop with the nostalgia right now and get back to "words" (. . . even though nostalgic is how I would describe the traditional real estate agent).

Like it or not, if you are a real estate agent, broker or any other real estate business professional where 'selling' is required, you should know that you are in the marketing business. You can claim you are in the real estate business, but doing so damages your ability to really do amazing things with your business. Yes, you are in the marketing business.

I learned early on in my career that marketers make it their business to have what buyers want. To do that, they use 'words'. Words like . . . death. Words do mean things. The words you use, how well you use them, when you use them, who you use them on, all of it dictates how successful you will become, or unsuccessful you will be. In fact WORDS build highly profitable sales teams, as much as they keep agents as solo practitioners.

This book is not about words per se, but make no mistake about it, the USE of words, what you say, how you say them, how you use them, will either quantum leap your business into a highly profitable sales team OR cause a slow death of your real estate business.

There are a lot of things that die, cease to exist, are no more. When we say "death of the traditional real estate agent", we are referring to the WAY super successful real estate businesses are actually built. Make no mistake about it, this death has been taking place for quite some time and will continue to do so. It is inevitable, this death of the traditional real estate agent.

You have probably heard the same stats I have heard: like the fact that 80% of agents quit the business within a few years of getting into it. Or that 95% of agents make under $100,000 a year in income. But what about the super successful? Those making $500,000, $1 Million, $3 Million or more a year selling real estate? What do you hear or know about them . . . about those kinds of real estate agents businesses? What do you *really* know about them, how they think about things, why they reject industry norms and standards, why they are different? Perhaps you did not know that they are different, think differently, approach the business differently. If you didn't, you will absolutely discover that as you read this book.

From simple study we know they have lots of referrals, returning clients, mounds of testimonials, do more and more of the big numbers of transactions *and* they are rich. The reason they garner so much success is simple . . . they do an overall better, more consistent job at getting MORE buyers and sellers what they want than the traditional real estate agent. This is simply my opinion, but it is an opinion based on over two decades of experience and discovery. And

Up to 50 Transactions
Small Team Organizational Chart

Unlicensed Assistant

Office Manager/
Call Coordinator/
Team Courier/
Database Manager (Tech Support)

Rainmaker
YOU
Outside Sales Agent/
Inside Sales Agent/
Customer Service
Manager

when you analyze these teams, you discover they are able to accomplish so much success because they have a team, or is it that they have a great team because they have so much success?

A real estate sales team as we will define it here in this book is one that has a team leader (the Rainmaker) and team members, each with a specific role to play in getting business and satisfying the demands and needs of the clients. Done well, these teams are highly profitable and provide better service and results than the average, traditional agent can provide.

We will go about proving that to you as both fact and as trend. In Michael Gerber's words, "if your business depends on you, then you don't have a business, you have a job". So in order to get your business to a point where it does not depend on you, it's certain that a great team will be in place.

Restated, "If your real estate business depends on you, then you don't have a real estate business, you have a job". So if you get sick, and a buyer for one of your listings wants to see it . . . if it's just you, well that buyer goes elsewhere and your seller suffers. If you have any business at all and it's just you, this problem of "just you" is magnified and your clients indeed suffer. Craig Proctor says it like this: "If you try to be all things to everybody you will dilute your effectiveness."

I am including three illustrations of Teams. When you look at them, you will see the natural evolution of a growing real estate business. The more business you have, the more your need for people to help you, systems to make it all work smoothly, and technology to make it all work together, simultaneously. All of that will be discussed and disclosed in this book.

If you were to spend two days at one of our Platinum Millionaire Agent Maker Conferences, you would be surrounded by hundreds of Team Leaders/Rainmakers. All of them ambitious to grow, expand their already successful real estate businesses to levels that the vast majority of agents will never ever see. They have discovered that the Team System is a superior way of actually doing business, giving better service and results to their clients, and making more money. It is, after all, the preferred way of doing business in just about any industry.

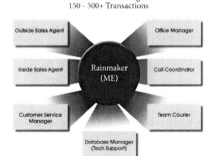

There is no stopping this trend. More and more teams will come, garner more market share, get paid premium fees, whether they operate within a franchise, as my mentor and coach Craig Proctor did, or on their own as an independent real estate sales team business. So make way for the Super Successful, Highly Profitable Real Estate Sales Team. If you don't make way, you will most likely get run over.

Go Sell Big!!!

Todd Walters

Preface

WHAT IS SUCCESS?

by Craig Proctor

How would you define a successful and enjoyable career in real estate? I would describe it this way:

- You have a steady stream of clients who automatically seek out your valuable services without you having to do any cold prospecting
- You are viewed with respect by clients who value your advice
- You are able to easily provide them superior service and results which leads them to refer you to others and give you their repeat business
- You work a normal work week (or less), and take plenty of time off to pursue outside interests
- You make a rewarding income

How many of you could describe your real estate career in this way?

The trouble in this industry is that the "hours worked = compensation" equation has traditionally been an "either / or" situation. In other words, you EITHER make a lot of money and have no life outside your job, OR you do have a life outside real estate but don't make enough money.

What's worse, for many agents, the equation is entirely unbalanced. There are many, many agents operating today who kill themselves with grueling 80+ hour weeks AND barely make enough money to survive. Maybe this even describes you.

According to the National Association of Realtors, 80% of new agents do not make it through the first year. Just as daunting is the fact that more and more real estate veterans are packing it in because they're finding they just can't make what used to work, work anymore: they're working far too hard to justify what's left in their pocket at the end of the day.

Why is this? Well, part of the problem is that the real estate market is changing so dramatically:

- consumers are more sophisticated and demanding
- commissions are under pressure
- technology is completely changing the way we do business, and
- more and more mega-agents are capturing a larger and larger market share

In the last decade, the number of agents operating in North America has dropped almost in half. Who will survive in the long term? Well, surely not the solo agent who's slugging it out by him or herself, burning the candle at both ends. They may shine brightly for a certain period of time, but sooner or later they'll run out of wick to burn, and then they'll simply burn out (they may win the sprint, but they can't do the marathon). Others run out of gas even before seeing success. Either way, this "model" of work-like-a-mad-dog is wrong.

Why did you get into real estate in the first place? I'll tell you why. Because you imagined that it would give you the freedom and cash to be able to live the lifestyle you wanted. But what has really happened?

Well, if you're like most agents, you're a slave to all the little details you have to accomplish. You know there are bigger issues and ideas out there that could improve your life, but you just don't have time to get to them, and before your eyes, another day, month, year has passed you by. And you're still working way too hard.

How satisfied are you with the money you make and the hours you work? At the end of the day, how much time is left over for you and your family?

The problem is that your real estate career, which was supposed to support your life, has now consumed your life. The job which was supposed to give you freedom is doing the very opposite -- it's taking your freedom away. This is wrong! All perspective is lost. You're just a rat on the wheel who's going to wake up one day and wonder how you can possibly be stuck in the same old place when you've been running so incredibly hard.

The problem is, you're looking at it all wrong. You're stuck in a paradigm which says "this is the way it is . . . there's no other way".

But there is another way. That's why we wrote this book. We want to shine the light on . . . a different way -- a better way -- to run your business so that it grows and thrives and feeds you (rather than bleeds you.)

You must change your paradigm to survive

The pages of this book are packed full of gold nuggets, direction, clues, specifics and most importantly PROOF OF RESULTS. Proof that what I am telling you here is possible. But before you can start this process of change or accepting change, you need to open up your mind to new ways of conducting your business and make a paradigm shift that will help you understand how to make your business serve your needs. And before you can do this, you're going to have to discover what those needs are . . . what your true needs are.

Let's get started . . .

✦ ✦ ✦

WHY WE CAN WRITE THIS BOOK . . .

by Todd Walters

You have probably heard of the "Franchise Prototype", or at least words like that. I first heard those words as it relates to a successful real estate business back in the mid 90's from Craig Proctor. You never really forget something that changes your way of life.

Way back in 1993, I developed a belief that I could make $1 Million a year or more selling real estate; this after some semi successful three years in the business. I was making right around $100K selling real estate at that time; selling mostly HUD homes and other buyer transactions. Any listings I was getting were due to the buyers having a house to sell.

Needless to say, I still thought there was something more to this business, a lot more in fact. So I figured the fastest way for me to succeed was to find someone to copy. I could try to figure it out on my own, or I could copy someone doing what it was I wanted to do.

Before I get too deep into all that, let me share with you my personal story that will have some golden nuggets for any ambitious agent.

In 1989 I was desperate. I was coming off a three year failed pizza delivery business. The pizza store was a franchise that I talked my Dad into going into business with me, and talked my Grandmother into loaning me the money to buy. Oh, I remember it well. My Grandmother loaned me

$40K (to be repaid at 10% interest) and My Dad dug up another $10K (and, I am sure, gave his Mother the assurance of keeping an eye on me). That $50K allowed me to purchase this Pizza Franchise in NW Metro Atlanta and begin my young entrepreneur career.

About one year in to this venture, I realized that I had, in essence, bought myself a job: I had borrowed and invested $50K to buy myself a job paying me somewhere around $30K a year. Three years into this venture, it was clear it was not going to work, or rather I was not going to be able to make it work the way I thought it should. So I did what many do when other business ventures/ jobs, don't work out: I got my real estate license.

Now let me frame this for you. I am 21 years old, I owe my Grandmother $40K plus 10% interest and I've got my Dad looking to recover some of his investment. AND I am in big time debt with credit cards, etc.

I needed to sell the house I had bought a couple years earlier because I could not make the payments. Here's some good news: the mortgage I had was an FHA Non Qualifying Non Escalating Assumable Loan: meaning that a buyer could simply assume the loan without having to qualify to do so. All I needed to do was sign it over to the new buyer.

The ad I ran in the real estate section of the paper went something like this:

Awesome NENQ Assumable. $3500 Down, $787 a month.
Blah, blah blah about the house. Call Todd at 000-000-0000.

I had 25 or so calls on that ad, and the second buyer through the door bought the house.

The real story is that I ran this ad for another 2 years.

Here's why. I had to tell over 20 buyers that the house was no longer available, but if they'd like, I could prepare a list of homes for them with NENQ Assumable loans they could buy with less than $5K down.

Bottom line I had accidentally offered something to the real estate market that it wanted and wanted really badly. At least a certain segment of it anyway.

Understand I was a brand new agent, selling my own home due to no income, failing Pizza business, eating lunch at the gas station using my gas credit card, living in my father-in-law's basement after quickly selling my house. But . . . I had stumbled onto something that SOME of the buyers in my market wanted: a house with a loan they could assume and not have to worry about qualifying for a mortgage to buy.

When I joined the RE/MAX Office after getting my license, the Broker/Owner told me to go partner up with another agent in the office in a similar situation as me - new and no business.

That agent simply suggested we grab the phone book and start cold calling. After three days of that, I called a young lady that had worked for me at my Pizza Place and offered her the job of telemarketing. I was pretty busy following up with the leads I was getting from my little NENQ classified ad on my own personal home, so it seemed like a good idea. I paid her with my credit card for about the first month until the two deals she did get from cold calling closed. This enabled me to pay off my credit card, but shortly after that she quit.

I severed the relationship with the guy I sort of partnered with and doubled down on the little NENQ ad I was running. Each time the ad ran, I would get 15 to 20+ buyers to call. I was successful within my first 6 months of selling real estate, making in excess of $40K.

One little classified ad, offering to the market place what it wanted (or at least what a significant niche wanted) had, in effect, launched my real estate career.

You see, I could have simply run the ad the first time, and as soon as an offer was secured on my home, told buyers the house was no longer available, making no further offer to them or making them a stupid offer like: 'That home is sold, I am an agent, can I help you find something else . . .'

But, fortunately, I did not know any better and made them an offer for something they actually wanted, a FREE LIST OF HOMES MATCHING THEIR EXACT CRITERIA, playing off the fact that I had access to just such properties, was an expert at those kinds of homes and loans because I was, in effect, owner of/former owner of one.

The gold nugget here is to **ONLY offer to your prospects what it is they want, whether you have it or not.**

I spent the next couple years doing well working with buyers, trying to figure out what it was they wanted and offering it via ads in the newspaper. Really getting by on my own hustle.

Like I said earlier though, in 1993 I realized there had to be a better way. In fact, I felt that with my work ethic and motivation to get out of debt and out of my father-in-law's basement, I could really do well.

I wanted to make $1 Million or more, felt it was possible selling real estate, even though NO ONE in GA was close to such a thing. And therein lies another gold nugget. **I looked around at what it was most agents were doing in my home state (market area) and concluded NOT**

to do it that way. Since no one was making $1 Million or even close, it was only logical that I better stay away from everyone here.

Fortunately I was a RE/MAX agent and in 1992 learned that the #1 RE/MAX agent in the U.S. made over $1 Million in commissions. So I leveraged my RE/MAX connection and called him up.

His name was Marshall Redder. His hometown was Grand Rapids, MI. My call to Marshall went something like this: Hello Marshall, My name is Todd Walters and I am a RE/MAX agent down here in Metro Atlanta, I think I can make $1 Million like you and want to know if it's OK if I come up to Grand Rapids for a couple days and you show me how to do it?

And there is another Gold Nugget for you: **Find super successful people, doing what it is you want to do and go hang out with them.**

Marshall said to come on up 'for a fee'. I borrowed the money from my Mom and flew up to Grand Rapids, spent 2 days with Marshall Redder, #1 RE/MAX Agent in the U.S. for 1992.

I learned some really great stuff from Marshall, like never stop running ads that work . . . ever. Also learned a little bit about a USP (Unique Selling Proposition), but the one BIG thing I learned was WHO *he* was hanging out with.

Over the two days with Marshall, he kept talking about a guy in Canada named Craig Proctor. He said Craig was doing even better than he was and was going to be the #1 RE/MAX Agent Worldwide that year.

I took what I learned from Marshall and put it to work in my business upon returning home from those two days in 1993. I added $100K or so to my business income the following year as a result, but the BIG thing I got from Marshall was that HE thought Craig was someone to associate with.

Later in 1994, I contacted Crag Proctor's office and used the same script I used on Marshall when I called him. Craig said he had just released his business system in a box that I could purchase, called the Quantum Leap System.

Of course I whipped out the credit card and bought it. It cost well over $1K I remember. And there is another gold nugget for you. Successful people, real true successful people, will share with you details about their business, but you must expect to pay for it. Moreover, successful people value what it is that has made them successful. And if indeed it is valuable - pay for it.

Oh yea, and . . . I came to realize that **successful people evaluate opportunity NOT for what it will cost, but for what they will gain.**

A year after buying and implementing some of what I had learned from Craig's Quantum Leap System, I had added close to an additional $75K to my real estate business. I had a buyer's agent and an assistant. I was now making around $250K in commissions, roughly 5 years into my real estate career. It was about this time I got a letter from Craig inviting me to his Real Estate SuperConference.

I remember it well. I and my assistant flew to Toronto and spent 2.5 days with Craig in a large conference room where he walked through his Franchise Prototype of his Millionaire Agent Real Estate Business.

It was at this time that I really began to see the business differently. Even though I was already much different than most agents in Metro Atlanta, Craig revealed to me a clear and concise road map for success.

Are you ready for this? Here it is . . . the secret to my success.

COPY and IMPLEMENT The Best!

You see, just a few years earlier I believed I could make a million dollars selling real estate. I set out on a quest to do that, to find the person I could copy and see to it that it happened. Craig had offered to let me copy him, detail for detail.

Of course he made the same offer to all of the couple hundred or so agents that were in the Royal York Hotel over those 2.5 days in 1995.

Little did I know that I would go on to become the guy who really, really did it and by all accounts do it (copy) better than any other.

Using Craig Proctor's Quantum Leap System, I went on to sell 400 - 500 homes a year, and was named one of the top 10 RE/MAX Agents worldwide. I was featured in books like Best Agent Business' book *The Billion Dollar Agent: Lessons Learned* and Dan Gooder Richard's early book on internet marketing *The Real Estate Rainmakers Guide to Online Marketing.*

In 2003, roughly $20+ Million in commissions earned later as a result of COPYING and IMPLEMENTING Craig's real estate business system, he asked me to help him launch what was to become one of the most successful real estate coaching programs in history: The Platinum Millionaire Agent Maker Program.

Over my tenure as Platinum Coach, I have had many, many agents come to me and say they too want to make $1 Million in commission, even NET $1 Million in commissions. My prescription for them, and for you, is to simply COPY what we teach you. The better you are at copying, the better you will be at seeing your goal attained.

With that, let me be clear: the hardest thing I do as the Platinum Coach is in actually getting members to COPY. It seems most somehow don't believe it's that easy; that they must put their own spin on it. That their business is different; their prospects/clients are more sophisticated or more affluent; that they're operating at a different time, or in a different culture, etc. etc.

Let me be even clearer on this subject: I was a Southern Boy, in debt, living in my father-in-law's basement, working in a major U.S. metropolitan Market, traveling to learn from and copy an agent from Newmarket, Ontario, Canada. So if I can do it, you can too. But we are well beyond proving. It is simply a fact that what we do, teach, show, give to ambitious agents, works.

During my tenure as Platinum Coach, I have watched as many members became the #1 agents in their respective markets, franchises, real estate companies. I've personally watched, and helped them, quantum leap their businesses to Millionaire and Multi-Millionaire Real Estate Agent Businesses. In fact, you will hear from some of these wildly successful agents throughout this book. What I want you to know is that these agents were/are the best at copying and implementing what we teach and give them.

Let me be super clear here, Craig Proctor IS THE GUY who brought much of what YOU hear about today from various sales gurus and real estate coaches to market. Examples would include The Team System, Inside Sales Agents, Outside Sales Agents, The Guaranteed Sales Program at the Agent Level, Performance Guarantees, Less Branded Direct Response Marketing and lots more.

Again, the better I was at copying Craig, the better my business grew, the more profitable I was and the happier my clients were. Same for the many in our coaching programs who did/do the same.

I have learned MUCH from Craig, way more than we can cram into a Real Estate Business Building Book. But there are three big things that stand out that I want to mention here.

In fact, these three big things you will see repeated throughout this book by myself, Craig and our contributing Authors.

THREE BIG THINGS I learned from Craig Proctor that allowed me to make HUGE quantum leaps in my business:

1. The Development and Implementation of a Unique Selling Proposition
2. Actually Using a Contact Management System

3.   The DISC Personality Concept Applied to SELLING and Growing
      Your Team.

Again, pretty much everything I know about being successful in this
business I learned from, or directly copied from, Craig, but these things
really stand out as early game changers. Again, these three will be revealed
in greater detail as you read and study this book.

As you turn the pages in this book the one BIG thing you will want
to know above all others, the one thing that makes ALL of this business
growth and super success possible, that you will want to accept as fact is
this:

To Grow Your Real Estate Business
You Must Have an Overflow of It

That's right . . . without an overflow of business (prospects, clients)
you will NOT be able to grow your business. It takes OVERFLOW (more
business than you/your team can get to) to facilitate growth.

Yes, it's true this scares many agents. But let me share with you a basic
fact that gets to the heart of this book.

Your buyers and sellers prefer to do business
with busy, successful agents

You and I are the same way. We drive by the restaurant that has no
cars in the parking lot and will wait an hour or more at the one that has
customers lining up out the door, standing in the parking lot waiting to
get in.

To handle the overflow of business, you will simply implement the
basic strategy of leverage. In fact, it's leverage that actually gets you an
overflow: leveraging yourself with marketing, people and technology. And
this premise describes Craig's Quantum Leap System.

To summarize WHY Craig and I can write this book . . . well, quite
simply, we have had enormous success establishing and leveraging a highly
profitable real estate sales team, at the top of the industry, for many years.
BUT, the real WHY is that we have taught countless others to do it as well.

Many of the chapters in this book are written by Super Successful,
Highly Profitable Real Estate Sales Team Leaders. Agents that believed
there was something more, wanted something more, came to Craig Proctor
searching for it. They are all members of our Private Mastermind group,

Titanium RE. Most were not at or even close to Millionaire Agent Status when I met them. But applying the systems, strategies and materials we teach and give them, they quickly established highly profitable real estate team businesses.

One other point about the co-authors of this book; they are from all over North America. This means that wherever YOU are, you too can quantum leap your real estate business into a super successful, highly profitable real estate sales team business. One that can work without your constant involvement, serving you rather than you serving it; delivering superior results and experiences to your clients.

Let's go sell Big!

Part 1

Chapter 1
Do you have a business
– *or just a job?*

by Craig Proctor

Hi, I'm Craig Proctor. You know me or know of me, and you may *incorrectly* think you know everything about me and know what I'm about. I am about raising yourself to Millionaire Agent status.

You came to this book for good reason. Now give me a chance to open your eyes and mind to realities about the real estate business, drawn from my 25 years of top-of-the-mountain experience. You're definitely going to read things here you do not expect. By the time you finish this book you may be shell-shocked. Or you may feel relieved and newly optimistic, realizing you've finally discovered a truth-teller. I want to get you to examine real estate differently than you ever have before. I promise, give me your time here, and I will reward you, directly, with value.

I asked: do you have a business you own – or *just a job that owns you?* I can also ask: which do you want? Getting to the west coast by heading east is *possible*, but you will need superhuman persistence to do it. Yet that IS exactly what most agents do. They say they want a business, but they stick with all the thinking and behavior of the mass numbers of agents who have nothing but hard jobs. And, mostly for their own reasons, they are ground like meat by coach after coach who keep them harnessed and plodding, with blinders on, focused just on The Work. There is actually a famous coach still laying on the whip, getting agents to make cold calls by phone. Partying as if it was 1999. Why anyone would pay good money every month to be told *that* is beyond me. It's like paying for lessons in blacksmithing or candle-making. Other coaches play at an opposite game, producing a next, new, shiny object every few months – as a distraction from the simple fact they've never produced a *business* *system* that works. But let's set all their charlatanism aside for now, and focus on this key issue and challenge: job OR business.

Real estate is actually a difficult, frustrating, disappointing and stressful job. Getting worse. Guaranteed to be harder in the future. If you have years in and earn a good income, you are probably asking yourself: *when does this get easier?* It doesn't. Ever. If approached as the commissioned salesperson worker doing a job. It stays the same. Every week a repeat of last week. It's a terrible job. Stop and think about how STRANGE the real estate agent situation is, in comparison to other fields. If you are a salesperson on commission for almost any Fortune 1000 company in any industry, you get a base or draw – a check *every* Friday, a company car, health insurance, a 401K, *and commissions*, and the company pays for all its own advertising, marketing, brochures, web sites, even for your business cards. You build up equity in accounts from which business comes to you *regularly.* You take 100% of your income out – you don't reinvest huge hunks of it. And if you're good, you make over $100,000.00 a year.

As a real estate agent, you have a job but everybody *pretends* it's a business.

You are told: it's just a numbers game. If you work harder and run faster, you win. There's no substitute for pressing the flesh, for networking, for open houses and taking buyers from house to house. Does this sound like being the owner of a business – or a worker in a sales *job?*

But what if real estate could be a terrific business?

What if we could eliminate cold calls of any kind. Eliminate demeaning beauty pageant auditions, making listing presentations to prospects also interviewing 4 other agents. Eliminate Tour Guide Duty. Never sit twiddling your thumbs at an Open House. Stop being on call 24/7 like a bail bondsman.

Top agents work with me and stick with me because they grasp the differences between having a lousy job or a great business. Lots of one trick pony and shiny object coaches have appeared and disappeared during my 25 years, while I sustained not only my top 10 ranking worldwide for RE/MAX but also grew my coaching business to one of the most successful in the world, helping to create and influence more 6-figure and 7-figure agents than anyone else. I absolutely understand the difference between having a lousy job and a great business. I made being a real estate agent into a real business and let it make me a millionaire running largely on auto-pilot, making money *for me*. **Nobody else on earth teaches *this*.** Those teaching and coaching, as well as some brokers, are all about keeping you focused on Doing The Work. Pushing you to Do More. Shaming you for Not Doing Enough.

Would you like to hear about that difference – and the reasons it is so important to you and your life, your marriage and family, your health and sanity, and your future?

Real success hangs in the balance.

I can marry your talent, ability, and experience with an entirely different and *very rare* approach. I call it ***The Millionaire Agent System***. I actually ***dare you*** to examine it and compare it to what you're doing now, and to what everybody else is telling you.

Let's dig in.

First, why do I say that being a real estate agent is such a terrible *job?* Well, it *does* own you. It is *not* 9 to 5, or 5 days and thank God it's Friday. Many of your friends, your spouse's friends and their husbands or wives have such jobs, including high-paying ones. They are free after 5 o'clock. Free on weekends. They can make plans and keep them. They can relax. They wonder what is wrong with you. Around them, you're never relaxed. Always anxious. Constantly saying "sorry – but I *have to* take this." They see you getting your leash pulled by an unseen hand. Behind your back, they feel sorry for you or mock you. Everyone around you CAN see: you do NOT own a business. You have a lousy job. And you live in fear of loss. Even if you earn a good income, admit it: you are living in fear. You can't afford to let even one prospect get away. One deal fall apart. You are jumpy and jittery. And, of course, there are the work hours and the mostly unproductive work itself. If you sit at open houses, *hoping*…..if you still cold call or have others cold calling for you….if you still play tour guide…. if you give listing presentations to people interviewing five other agents, people who do not respect you, people who try negotiating fees with you … and, most importantly, if you feel that you must re-start the engines every day; that you have to get out there and find and hunt for business; if you have no certain in-flow of clients … then you have a bad job. A BAD JOB.

If that makes you mad and defensive, hold on. It's <u>not</u> *your* fault you're in the mess you're in, that brought you to this book. There is literally a vast and well established conspiracy to keep agents thinking and acting like employees in bad jobs yet spending out of their own pockets on advertising, marketing, training, coaching and more as if they owned businesses. You don't have to admit to any personal malfunction to consider my very different approach. You just have to admit to the restless wondering why you must keep working so damned hard. I happened to hear an old commercial on a recording of a radio broadcast from 1951 the other day. The ad was for the Blue Coal Company. It was all about a magical new device called a 'thermostatic regulator' that could control your furnace, running on coal in the basement, and liberate you from running up and down the stairs twenty times an evening to fiddle with the damper when it got too hot or too cold upstairs. Of course, you still had to go down now and then to shove more coal in. This is how people lived. This is how most agents live. There is no fully automated, fully integrated system bringing them a certain and steady flow of good clients. There is, instead, endless running down and up the steps to shovel in coal and adjust the damper by hand.

Exchanging an out-dated approach for a superior, modern system is <u>not</u> admission of failure. Really smart people do this a number of times during their business careers. Buffett has recently, dramatically reduced his stock-picking and stock-owning in favor of much more outright ownership and running of companies – most recently by trading his $4-billion of stock in Proctor & Gamble for 100% ownership of their division, Duracell. Bezos started Amazon as an online bookstore. We've all moved a hunk of advertising from newspapers to Craigslist, Google, and Facebook. Please don't cling to a coal furnace. Don't stubbornly defend your coal furnace. Don't be emotional about this. Ego is the enemy of progress. Force your mind open. Oh, and don't be fooled by youth, inexperience and razzle-dazzle either. Just because somebody is half my age, dresses trendy, and pours money into being flashy, does *not* mean *they* have *anything* new. Most of the cool kids in coaching were students of mine to start with, and are mostly teaching Craig Proctor 1.0, diluted and re-labeled. And they are actually BEHIND what I'm doing. Anyway, let's keep on track here.

A minute ago, I used the word: career.

Sometimes people call real estate a *career*. Nonsense. Careers have progressive, ascending career paths. You start in one place and climb up a career ladder. No such thing here. And there's no reward here for patience either.

Others say they are in business, but businesses function *for* their owners. *The owner of* ten Wendy's restaurants does not get up every morning making cold calls or handing out flyers or going to networking meetings *hoping* to entice somebody to come in and buy a burger. Nor does he get behind the counter and cook the burgers. **If you are doing the repetitive manual labor in the business you are <u>not</u> the owner of a real business**. If anything, you are owned by it. Don't kid yourself and don't let yourself be kidded. Business cards, a web site, a fancy Powerpoint presentation are *not* a business. Being nothing more than a commission sales agent beating the bushes is <u>not</u> a business.

Many call being a real estate agent a business but theirs isn't. There *can* be a real estate agent *business*, but most aren't, and bluntly, yours probably isn't. The guy with the five Wendy's, the owner of shoe stores, the owner of the small manufacturing firm that makes nozzles for bottles sold at Wal-Mart <u>knows</u> that some number of customers will come through the doors or some number of orders will arrive each week because there is Perpetual Motion in these businesses. They run by *system*. Yes, the money flow varies a little week to week, month to month. A little. Up a little, down a little. But just a little. It is steady and predictable. These businesses produce income *for* their owners. If yours doesn't, it isn't really a business at all.

When somebody finally admits this truth to themselves, after denying it to self and others for years, it can be pretty traumatic and dramatic. If you have been growing your income by running faster, working harder, even working smarter, but not growing any EQUITY, you've fallen into a trap. The only possible way to create a business out of this is by SYSTEM --- a real, complete system that gets clients for you, mostly automatically, and predictably, with reassuring constancy, and by having a team and circle of people in orbit around you, who function without micro supervision or daily breath blowing, because of the SYSTEM. I've conquered both those things.

When people realize they are in jobs and not in business, sometimes the shock causes exodus.

Many professionals are opting out of income uncertainty and surrendering, officially, to jobs. Dentists, for example, are, in droves, selling their practices – in truth, jobs, not businesses – to big corporate chains and then going to work for them as employees. 9 to 5, free every weekend, 2 weeks paid vacation, 401K, and a steady paycheck brought home every Friday, the same known-in-advance amount written on it every time. Why? When people realize and admit they have jobs not businesses, they weary of having *bad* jobs. They get sick and tired of the worry and anxiety of income uncertainty. As you have or will. Defending yourself to spouse, family, friends. Apologizing for being called away, on call, for gulping dinner then going back out to a listing presentation, later slinking home empty-handed and disappointed.

I don't want you to surrender. I don't want you to stay in this thing as you are and as everybody else does it either.

So, let me lay out, pure and simple, my proposition: with my Millionaire Agent System, you will actually own a real business and *as its CEO*, you will get a very fine salary, work 9 to 5 with your evenings free and your weekends free. You can even leave your cell phone off and ignore your email for an entire weekend. Heresy, I know, but get ready to amaze your spouse. You'll get many weeks of paid vacation, without angst and worry and being jittery. Good benefits. Build up a fat 401K and own a pension. Instead of rising each morning to go forth as nervous hunter with club and pointed stick in search of your family's next meal, you will be a business owner, with a business providing that meal for you, thanks to the functioning of its System.

And I'm not done. *Wait. There's more.* This System will also lift you above and set you apart from all competition. Finally, you'll get a stay above the fray. If it grinds your gears that you are constantly competing as if equal with far less experienced, capable and successful agents, **The Millionaire Agent System** fixes that. If you are still having your time wasted or stolen by un-serious prospects shopping around for *an* agent, now you will deal only with prospects pre-determined to have you as *the* agent. My *Millionaire Agent System* doesn't just transform a bad job into a great business, it changes for the better the relationship between you and your clients, and, ultimately, between your team and the clients.

Finally, further, my System will make your business secure and sustainable. There are negative trends and forces. There is actually a shrinking number of buyers. A great many agents are going to starve out in the near future. My System can insulate you from this. Before it's too late.

Let's talk briefly about **how you can *lose everything*** and have your income yanked right out from under you like a tablecloth whipped out from under a table full of dishes by a magician. It has happened. It's going to happen again. It happens to agents who are over dependent on any one source or means of getting clients. Committed to *a* shiny object. In 2004, I had to run full-page ads aimed at agents, headlined: "CALL A FSBO, GO TO JAIL", because the do-not-call list law took effect. Agents lost licenses, paid huge fines. Still happens. Many agents suddenly had no income and no skills or system for having any, because they had believed that making such cold calls would never be taken away from them. Fast forward to 2015: recently, President Obama announced that he intends to re-classify the internet as a communications utility, like TV, and have it regulated by the FCC, even though it is already regulated by the FTC. But the FCC regulates content. Imagine having to function with a big catalog of forbidden words and phrases for your web sites, Facebook site, emails and so on. Imagine the subject line required for every email you send being: Advertisement From Real Estate Agent.

Listen carefully. I have lived long and prospered. If you let yourself become overly dependent on any one means of obtaining clients, you place yourself *in peril*. In danger. You should never sleep peacefully. If you are overly dependent on the internet, look out. Google and Facebook and Craigslist are, themselves, regulatory bureaucracies that can and do change the rules by their whim, without warning. I'm NOT saying we don't use every online opportunity – we do. But we have a much, much more complete system, so that changes in any one thing do not affect us like a dynamite blast. My friend Dan Kennedy has a saying: stability can only come from diversity. Or, if you hop around from one shiny object, one easy button to the next like a flea on Starbucks hopping from dog to dog, you might land on the wrong dog – just as disruption occurs. My System brings order and discipline, manageable diversity and flexibility, multiple streams of clients functioning for you simultaneously. There's nothing else like this System, period. It's like a Peyton Manning offense. You have to see it to fully appreciate it. When you do, you see it as an impressive work of art and as a unique demonstration of science and engineering. It is so far from the running around randomly advertising, prospecting and selling that dominates most agents' lives, and that most coaches teach, it might as well be from another plant, like Superman, an alien from outer space.

I *can* help you transform your real estate *job* into a real estate *business*. If you can copy, you can succeed. The contributing authors in this book, all of them students of mine, are proof that this system does work to transform the lives of agents from all marketplaces, backgrounds, starting points and circumstances. What are you waiting for?

Chapter 2
There's No Money
in Real Estate

by Todd Walters

Strange, Weird, And Controversial PROOF There is NO MONEY in REAL ESTATE – BUT a Whole Pile of it for YOU in Marketing!!!

Part One: What business are you really in?

As stated earlier in this book, the correct answer is *The Marketing Business*!

Marketers make it their business to have what the marketplace wants. So **the focus should be on the prospect, not on the agent.** There is a big difference.

Most agents confuse advertising with marketing. Let me explain in more detail. Back when I first got into real estate, I wondered what it would be like to make a million dollars selling real estate. The harder I worked at selling real estate, the more I knew I would NEVER see $1Million in income doing it that way. Fortunately for me, shortly after getting into real estate, I met Craig Proctor, through a RE/MAX agent named Marshal Redder, in 1992.

I approached Marshal because he had made over $1 Mil that year, so I called him and asked if I could come visit. I told him I wanted to learn from him for a couple days because I wanted to do the same thing in my market of Metro Atlanta. But the whole time I was there in Grand Rapids with Marshall, he kept talking about this guy in Toronto, Canada.

That next year, Craig Proctor was named the #1 RE/MAX agent worldwide, bringing in well over $1 Million in commissions. So I called Craig's office and invited myself to a conference he was having.

It was there that I learned what business he was in, what business I needed to be in and what business ALL successful top producers were in – the Marketing Business. Specifically, Direct Response Marketing. You see, **the kinds of advertising I engaged in prior to this made all sorts of boasts about me, but it really offered no benefits to prospects.** The advertising I did was the same kind of ineffective advertising most agents do to this day. Meaningless boasts about themselves saying – here I am, a Real Estate Agent and I can help you buy or sell . . . Craig Proctor, 15 consecutive years in the Top 10 for RE/MAX Worldwide taught me that EFFECTIVE marketing:

- talks *to and about your prospects*
- gives prospects *real benefits*
- gives prospects a *non-threatening way to get more information*, and
- gives prospects *compelling reasons* to contact you to get it

I now teach agents this as the Platinum Coach with Craig Proctor Coaching. You see, you can't **make** prospects call you. Prospects won't call you just because you want them to. They won't call you just because they are aware that you exist. **They will only call you if it will benefit them in some way.**

Most agents think to attract prospects you have advertise yourself, get your name out there, build your brand, but they are sadly mistaken. **The purpose of marketing is to ATTRACT prospects - NOT promote yourself.**

As soon as you learn to STOP being a Real Estate Agent Selling Houses to Buyers and Sellers and START being a Marketer of Solutions for Those Wanting to Buy or Sell, the sooner you will discover the key to really making money in real estate.

Part Two: The Critical Areas of Your Real Estate Business You Should be Focusing On to Ensure a Long and Prosperous Career!

I often get asked from members in the Platinum Program "What should I focus on?" The answer is pretty simple, but also a bit detailed: whatever works to grow your profits.

Michael Gerber calls them Rainmaker activities. We believe there are only 3 ways for you to grow your real estate business:

1. Increase the number of transactions.
2. Increase the size of the transaction income.
3. Increase the number of times Clients come back and buy from you.

Where do MOST of your transactions come from? Better asked, where do most transactions of Millionaire Agents Come From? Remember, to be successful, copy success!!

Most transactions come from CLIENTS! A client is a buyer or seller who signed an agreement to work with you exclusively. So to increase transactions, increase the number of clients. BUT, as I said, the details are a bit complex because MOST agents struggle in this area.

First, you don't want EVERY or ANY client. You want those who you identify with, that believe YOU are the one to help them and value your services. You know exactly what I am talking about. We all have had Clients that were downright mean, rude, disrespectful – no matter what you did right. At the end of the day, you would be better off without these types because they rob you of precious energy and these types take up too much time, meaning you make less money.

Before I go on about these 3 areas of focus, let's address MONEY, or better yet, income. The purpose of your business is to produce a profit. The more the better. But some agents are squeamish about making money. Quick to discount or cut commissions at the slightest push back from a prospect. You need to know this is a wealth creation inhibitor. You are morally obligated to get as much money as you can. Here's why; the majority reading this will reinvest the majority of what they make back into their business by hiring more people to leverage, investing in more and better technology and marketing. You have a sensational desire to GROW your business. All of these spending measures lead to greater services and usually better results for your clients. Better results for clients means MORE income for you. So when I say "make more money" – it is assumed you understand that in order to do that, you must provide exceptional value to prospects and clients first . . . and then the money almost magically appears.

So ALL benefit – you, your family, your employees and of course your customers. More Money is GOOD as it provides great leverage to pursue opportunities. So don't be squeamish.

This leads me to number two on the list of areas of focus: increase the amount of money you make per transaction.

Most agents think this means selling a more expensive house, since most get paid a percentage commission. That may be fine, but what if homes in a higher price range are in low demand and not selling? It makes no sense to have 20, $500,000 listings if buyers don't want them, but instead want $175,000 homes. A good way to go broke in a hurry is by pursuing real estate NOT in demand, and a good example of being IN the real estate business instead of being IN the Marketing Business.

Most agents simply charge whatever they are charging because "that's the way ALL the other agents do it". BUT – remember, agents are not your clients, or even your prospects. In fact, last time I checked most agents are broke or going out of business. The statistics say that 80% fail and get out of the business within a few years of getting into it, so I sure would NOT be doing what the majority are doing.

This does not mean you should be ignorant of competition and pricing. Your job is to BEAT your competitors by providing a better value. Start by testing your prospects. On your next listing appointment you could ask for 0.5% more or work up in 0.25% increments. Until you get push back that is a diminishing return. When that begins to happen, add on MORE value to justify the fee. To do that, demonstrate results.

Sellers will pay more to the agent who has buyers. So make sure that on your next listing appointment you take along a list of BUYERS you have in your database who are looking for real estate. Demonstrate that YOU are The Agent with Buyers. There are many agents out there with MORE buyers than you in their database, BUT that means nothing unless it's marketed, demonstrated, proven.

What about number three, increasing the number of times a prospect returns and buys from you? How does that factor in? Well, it's no secret that the average buyer will return in 7.5 years to make another move. That is a long time to wait and probably NOT worth your time to stay in touch to ONLY pursue their return. MUCH better to stay in touch but with a different offer altogether in this area.

I teach Platinum Members to pursue referrals from their past clients with a very specific and exclusive referral marketing system, leveraging a worthy cause. In fact, I publish a newsletter each month that Platinum Members use to get more referrals. If you do this right, then when your past client is ready, they will refer themselves to you. But getting referrals really falls into the category of increasing the number of transactions.

Getting clients to come back and buy is about either referring themselves to you when they are ready to make a move, AND actually buying OTHER real estate from you, like investment property.

One of the other things I teach Platinum Members is to Position Themselves as Wealth Builders: Helping Past Clients Increase their Wealth By Investing in Real Estate. I dedicate another Monthly Newsletter to this topic exclusively, that I call "Position Marketing News".

One simple way to do this would be to send a killer deal on a home to your past clients each month telling them such and letting them know this is perfect for those wanting to increase or build wealth by investing in Real Estate. Invite them in for a one-on-one consult about buying real estate as part of a long term wealth creation strategy.

Doing this will absolutely position you as an expert, wealth builder, and authority on the subject of real estate. This elevates the likelihood of getting referrals from the past client, of having them refer themselves and coming to you to buy more real estate.

So there are THE 3 areas of focus, the ONLY 3 ways to grow your real estate business. If you can combine all 3 at the same time, you are well on your way to making a "quantum leap" as my long time mentor, Craig Proctor, would say.

Part Three: The Single Greatest Skill YOU Can Master as a Real Estate Agent to Guarantee Long Term Success.

I should just say: become a better marketer and move on to the next part, but that would leave you in the lurch. So I want to focus on THREE examples that I think will really help you GET this.

The first would be an example of lead generation skills. Remember, in order to grow your business you need an overflow of it. To generate an overflow of leads, you need MAGNETS! The type of magnet will depend on the kind of leads you want.

Back in 2005, I received a call from Craig Proctor who told me there was a company right here in my market that he believed would be worth talking to; that there may be a relationship that could be mutually beneficial, as he put it. At that time, I had sold close to $1 Billion in real estate sales thanks to listening to Mr. Proctor, so I contacted the gentleman he told me to call, Duane Legate with House Buyer Network.

House Buyer Network was generating between 10,000 and 20,000 motivated sellers a month with their EXCLUSIVE online marketing systems. The idea was that if it was really good, maybe we could strike up a referral relationship with one of our Coaching Programs. Duane agreed to let me test these leads for myself in my own business, to see if they were for real. We agreed to a two month test run where HBN would send over the Motivated Seller Referrals it was generating from www.HouseBuyerNetwork.com and I would pursue the seller as a client

It was less than two weeks later that I called Craig up and said these were some of the best leads I had ever gotten, especially in the MUST SELL YESTERDAY category. I went on to make close to $1 Million in commissions with HBN before selling my real estate company a few years later.

So you could say that HBN was a Motivated Seller Magnet. But it wasn't necessarily their website, it was the way it was marketed. In fact, the demand was so great for their service among members in our Platinum Program, HBN had to create a Motivated Seller Landing Page, that I coined Listings By Noon (LBN) so agents could run their own marketing and drive traffic to the LBN site.

The key here is the niche. HBN and LBN are set up to attract ONLY sellers who MUST sell and are super desperate to do so. They would not work well when targeting sellers who are not in a big rush, or see other alternatives. A business principle here is **if you try to be all things to all people, you will dilute your effectiveness.**

So be SOMETHING for SOMEONE

Another example would be to become an expert at converting prospects to clients. For most agents, this means developing a good buyer and seller benefits presentation, so when you get face to face you can pop open your laptop and give them a listing presentation that is unparalleled! And you should do that, but what if you could turn the prospect into a "come list me", before you even showed up? What would that do for your business? In 2003, I got a call from Craig Proctor that I remember vividly because it was the beginning of a game-changer for my business, and so many others we touched/touch.

Here is the conversation:

"General, what are you doing?" asks CP. "Well, I am in IL, outside shooting my bow," says I.

"How many leads did you generate last month," asks CP. "Around 1,000 or so," say I.

"And how many homes did you sell?"

"Around 50," I say.

"Isn't it a shame to have to generate 1,000 leads a month to only sell 50 homes a month?" says CP, so boldly.

Then he goes on to say that wouldn't it be great if we could just generate a lead, then send them something so profound, so impactful, that the prospect would call up and say "COME LIST ME".

I, of course said, yeah, that would be a game-changer. So Craig went to work on creating what we called the BOMB. It worked. We generate a lead, send the BOMB, and the lead calls up and says, come list me. It was indeed a game-changer on many, many levels. First of course, is the obvious. Next is that we got better prices on the listings AND higher commissions, less objections to both.

OK, one more example for you on skills, specifically becoming a better marketer.

It was 2007, and my listing inventory had ballooned from 125 active listings on any given day to over 300. BUT, at this same time as you may know, the market in the U.S. had begun to slow, the housing bubble was bursting. Each month I had more and more NEW listings and less and less closings. I had LOTS of frustrated sellers and outside sales agents. So I did what any wise agent would do, I looked around for something or someone to copy. I called virtually every top agent I knew (and trust me, that is a lot) and asked if they knew of any broker, agent, or company that sold every single listing, never having one expire. The consistent answer was, no. BUT, fortunately I had experience with the only ONE place that I believed could help me.

When I first jumped into real estate, I was flat broke and desperate. I ran an ad on my own home which had a NENQ (non-escalating, non-qualifying) FHA assumable mortgage loan on it. The ad was something like, "$3500 down and assume payment of $789 – do not have to qualify for a new loan, just take over payments and it's yours . . ."

I sold the house to one of the first buyers who looked at it, but had over 20 calls on that ad. Being a new agent, I offered all of those buyers a FREE list of ALL the other homes with the same kind of non-qualifying, assumable mortgage available matching their criteria. (Stumbled onto a great lead generating ad, a niche market). The loan was backed by

– yes, you guessed it – HUD; The Department of Housing and Urban Development.

I tell you this because almost 20 years later the answer to my question of . . . Who Never Has an Expired Listing, was . . . HUD. HUD sells everything. So then all I needed to do was to call my listings HUD homes. Problem was, I couldn't legally do that. So I set out to create a Sales Platform just like HUD.

Instead of calling my listings HUD homes, I called them RBID Homes. It was a magic pill and RBID saved my bacon. There are lots of lessons here for you. One, how can you create MORE demand for your listings over the other homes for sale, including Bank Owned Homes. Secondly, how can you make it fun and easy for Buyers to do business with you. And another is leverage; how can you create a system that generates a third party perception of sell and have buyers BID on the home at will.

Bottom line is RBID saved my bacon, but it was a whole host of experiences that allowed me to put something like that together, to have the mindset to do it.

Oh yeah, Duane Legate and the good folks at House Buyer Network built out the RBID system for me, and I in turn made it available to our Craig Proctor Platinum Members. As of this book writing, Lifestyle Media is now running the RBID system for our Platinum Program Members and it is still a great way to create a greater perception of value around an agent's listings.

Part Four: How to Escape the Inevitable Death of a Real Estate Agent

Such a morbid headline for this section, but an attention getter. And that leads me to the HUGE MISTAKE most agents are making, right now, that will undoubtedly KILL their careers. The headline above for this part took me about 5 seconds to dream up. Even though my lovely wife would NOT approve of my casual use of the phrase "DEATH of" . . . or of being overly confident enough to make such a headline. But I am not like the majority of agents, and in fact pride myself on that fact.

You must be willing to do things that OTHERS are not willing to do. As I sit here and type this, my 15 year old, High School Sophomore daughter is texting me, complaining about her late pm Strength and Conditioning lesson with her S&C Coach. It's scheduled for 7:30 pm. The reason for the late appointment is that the coach is good and busy. This was the only time she could get in today. You should also know that Morgan, my daughter, received scholarship offers to play Fast Pitch Softball even BEFORE her sophomore year ever started. She verbally committed to the University of Missouri. She had several offers to some awesome schools. Why did this happen? It is rare for athletes to be recruited at such a young age. But she is pretty darn good, she holds all the softball offensive records at her HS after only two years and led the state in her age group as a 14 and 15 year old in Home Runs. So yeah, she has talent. But like anything, talents will be taken away or lost if NOT put to use.

My experience is that MANY possess great talent. BUT few are willing to do the things necessary to leverage those talents. In the case above, with my own daughter, my text back was, "Continue to do the things your competitors are unwilling to do . . ."

OK, whatever, she's 15 and I "guilted" her into going. But it makes a good point about doing that which makes you successful:

- You must be willing to do what MOST are unwilling to do.
- Willing to test and split test your marketing.
- Willing to ASK for MORE commission.
- Willing to demand a transaction fee.
- Willing to MEET with buyers BEFORE looking at homes and present to them benefits of WHY they should work with you exclusively and agree to your fee.
- Willing to Work ON your business rather than in it all the time. Willing to hire slow but fire fast. Willing to demand results from all you do.

If you are not willing to do the things necessary for true success, then my friend, you will NOT find it. You will become like the majority, either out of the business or LESS than a six figure income, unable to HELP your clients at the level you want to, to elevate your own life or help your community. Working commission check to commission check. Sounds dire, deathly, grim.

Now you know why I can justify the headline of this section. I am writing all of this here because I want you to throw off the things that hold you back and move forward, as Craig Proctor would say, Quantum Leap Your Real Estate Business.

Part Five: How to Transition from Selling Real Estate to Marketer of Solutions for Those Wanting to Buy or Sell Real Estate

Marketing Guru Dan Kennedy calls it moving from the doer of your thing to the marketer of your thing. I think I have made a good case here for why you should adopt a paradigm of marketing instead of selling houses.

Here's an example of what I mean:

When a stranger comes up to you at a party and asks you "what do you do for a living . . ." what do you say?

Most agents say something like – 'I am a real estate agent' or 'I sell houses'.

And after saying that, get NO response or the typical small talk response of – "oh, ok, uh, great. So how's the market . . .".

A typical Member in our Platinum Millionaire Agent Maker Program would answer the question this way " . . . I guarantee the sale of houses and if the home does not sell, I buy it myself!"

Thus getting the response of "Holy #@&%, how do you do that?"

You see, once you graduate from being a real estate agent into a marketer of solutions for those wanting to buy or sell real estate – you are in demand. No more cold calling, no more manual grunt prospecting, no more of 'Oh, by the way', no more of that silly and unproductive stuff. Buyers and Sellers will seek you out. You have what they want. You are on your way to OVERFLOW and the need to leverage the overflow by growing your team.

Consider this ad:

Free Report Reveals 7 Costly Mistakes to Avoid
When Selling a Home in Alpharetta GA
(Mistakes that will cost you Tens of Thousands).
Call 1-800-000-0000 ID0000# for recorded info (talk to no agent)

- Do sellers in Alpharetta want to avoid mistakes? YES.
- Do they want to MAKE MORE MONEY when selling? YES.
- Do they want to talk to an agent? NO.

Sellers want buyers, buyers want sellers. So if you want either one, better give them what they want. This is how you transition. Learn how to become a Marketer of solutions to prospects you want to attract and avoid placing yourself into the 'mostly loser group' of real estate agents.

OK, now after such a fine short chapter in this book on a very solid topic, why did I have to go and say something like that. Well, it's true. MOST agents fail.

Fail themselves, their families, their obligations and their clients. Facing that truth is first and foremost so you will pledge NOT to do what the majority does and vow to be better. You become better by being different. Different is the operative word.

Being Different is what you should be discovering as you read this book.

Chapter 3
Selecting Your Target
Market and USP

by Craig Proctor

Who do you want to work with?
What do these people want?
How are you going to give it to them?

If you ask most agents who they are trying to target with their marketing efforts, they'll be a little vague in their response. Most agents probably feel they're after anyone and everyone in the hopes of attracting someone who is looking to buy or sell a home.

The problem with this strategy is that when you try to be everything to everyone, you fail to address the specific needs of anyone. If you're "targeting" everyone, your message is bound to be broad and unfocused, and is unlikely to be compelling and direct enough to draw in your prospect (whoever that is).

An unclear definition of who you're talking to with your marketing will lead to watered down statements that don't mean very much to anyone (such as "List with Me. I Care About Your Business." You may fool yourself with an empty statement like this, but you won't fool your prospects.)

Targeting is very important. It's important because it will determine where and how you should advertise and what you should say.

Step 1 of my system is really 3 mini-steps that you should be taking right now in your business. These steps are as follows:

1. Select Your Target Market

Are you after buyers or sellers? If you're after buyers, are you targeting: first time buyers or move-up buyers? If first time buyers are your target, a *Renters* editorial-style ad* is a great one to run. If you're more interested in move-up buyers, a *Trade-Up Mistakes* editorial-style ad effectively targets this group. My *6 Buyer Mistakes* editorial-style ad will draw both of these groups, as will most of the classified ads I share with agents I coach. *(*Note: These ads refer to a series of lead generation tools that come with my Quantum Leap System.)*

If you're after sellers (and you may well be interested in both buyers and sellers -- I certainly targeted both in my own business), the *Costly Homesellers* editorial-style ad and the *Find Out What the Home Down the Street* and *Distress Sale* classified ads, are jackpots in any market they run in.

But further than this, what kind of sellers do you want to work with:

* Owners of High-end properties?
* Owners of condominiums?
* Builders?
* Seniors?
* etc.

Maybe you want to target a very specifically defined geographic area such as:

* Waterfront
* Country Properties
* Specific Neighborhoods or towns
* etc.

Or do you want to work with all of these target markets? It's okay to target two or more different groups as long as you recognize that it's likely that each group will require different ads, so if you're going to go after multiple markets, make sure you understand the budget implications so you can properly launch and follow through on each plan.

The right answer to this question depends on you and the market you're operating in. How profitable and enjoyable is it to work with each of these groups from your perspective? How much inventory is there? How much competition? Do you have specialized knowledge and credibility in the defined target market or can you acquire it? How much money do you have to invest in the required marketing (of course, you should demand that each ad you run more than pay for itself - which you can measure specifically if you're running Direct Response advertising - which means that initial capital should not be an issue.)

If you need "now" business (i.e. if you not only don't have a lot of money to invest in your business but are actually starving for cash and need some NOW money), first-time buyers are the best way I know to generate quick cash. This group is easy to attract mainly because most other realtors don't have a profitable system to work with them, so they give up on first-time buyers. There's virtually no competition. I have found first-time buyers to be highly profitable. They're a jackpot.

In my experience, there's money to be made in most areas as long as you know what your customers want and how to give it to them. This leads me to the next two points.

2. Determine What Your Prospects Want

Again, ask yourself some important questions:

- "What motivates the target group of prospects that you're after?"
- "What factors are most important to them?"

Do they want a quick sale or top dollar? Are they after best value or most attentive service or least hassle? How do you find out what prospects want? Well, it's simple. You ask them. Failing to understand and address your customers' needs is one of the biggest marketing mistakes real estate agents make. Rather than assuming or guessing you know the answers, you should be asking your prospects directly by researching their needs. This doesn't have to be a complicated or time consuming task. I developed a simple but effective customer survey that I used to help me understand my prospects better.

3. Set Yourself Apart by Giving Your Prospects What They Want in a Unique and Innovative Way - (i.e. Develop your USP or Unique Selling Proposition)

This is a very critical part of the process, and you must read the next section very carefully. Your USP addresses a very important prospect issue - it answers the question: "Why should I do business with you?" You must have a very good answer to this question.

Why You Must Create a Compelling Usp

If someone asked you what made you different from all the other real estate agents in your marketplace - in other words, why they should choose you to buy or sell a home versus all other options - what would you say to them?

- Could you give them a compelling and convincing answer in 60 seconds or less?
- Would what you say elicit a response from them of, "Wow, how do you do that?"

Chances are your answer to both these questions is no, because the fact of the matter is, most real estate agents don't know what a USP (Unique Selling Proposition) is let alone have one. Sometimes, even if agents have a USP that they communicate in one-on-one situations (such as a listing presentation), they don't communicate it effectively to the masses in their marketing efforts. And yet, if you don't promote a compelling USP, you're not setting yourself apart from all of the other realtors in your marketplace.

Your USP tells the world who you are and what you do. It articulates clearly and concisely what benefit a prospect will derive from doing business with you instead of your competitors. You should be able to articulate your USP clearly in 60 seconds or less. Astonishingly, most realtors couldn't begin to clearly explain their USP at all, and if you can't articulate it, it's highly unlikely that your customers and prospects will be able to understand it.

The problem is that most realtors have never sat down and asked themselves these important questions:

- What distinguishes my company or business from my competitors?
- Do my homes sell faster? For more money?
- Do my buyers save money or time?
- Am I more expensive, less expensive?
- Do I have a better system to attract customers?
- Am I more aggressive in my marketing programs and strategies?
- Do I render more service? Give better value? Give a better guarantee? Make it easier to do business with me?
- What makes me different?

When it comes right down to it, most real estate agents don't have a USP at all. When I review the ads of most realtors, I invariably come across the same problems:

- There is no unique selling proposition, or
- There is a wandering statement that most frequently focuses on vague self-promoting generalities such as:

  o   we're #1
  o   we give the best service
  o   we have the lowest prices
  o   we're the biggest -- the best
  o   and so on

This is what I call 'Self Image Advertising'. The fact is, every company says the same old things and somehow expects them to be compelling . . .

- Quality
- Service
- Price
- Dependability

These same vague, broad promises are empty, meaningless, unsubstantiated, unbelievable and completely lacking in credibility. Yet still, everyone says them. Would you really expect anyone to claim that they give the worst service or offer the worst value?

In direct contrast to this, your USP must be benefit-driven. It must be meaningful, relevant and valuable to your prospects. Without these ingredients, your message will most likely fall on deaf ears. It won't be seen or heard. It will wind up getting "zapped" just like the thousands of other messages the average person is exposed to every single week.

Think About it From Your Customer's Perspective

An effective ad must be written from the prospect's standpoint, NOT the agent's. When you write an ad, INSTEAD of asking yourself: "What can I tell them about ME?" . . . you SHOULD be asking:

"What can I offer prospects that THEY want or need?"

All you have to do is scan your local paper to see that THE AVERAGE AGENT DOESN'T HAVE A CLUE about differentiating themselves. Everyone's saying the same bland old things or nothing at all. Most Real Estate agents waste their money on ineffective ads that produce little or no results other than possibly pacifying their sellers' demands by advertising their property.

Your Prospects Don't Care About You as Much as You Care About Them

Think of it this way. You probably have a pretty clear picture of your marketplace and the agents who compete against you. You scour every ad. Your ears are tuned to hear what's going on in the market. You solicit feedback on yourself and your competitors. You live and breathe your real estate business. In short, because you are so close to your business, you've entirely lost your objectivity - your perspective.

Well, let me tell you something very important. Your prospects couldn't care less. When your prospects decide to hire a real estate agent, the sea of choices looks just like that - a sea - a vast ocean of choices with no directional markers to steer his or her path to your door.

You know you're there. You know exactly who is operating inside this big body of water - who's fighting for position just underneath the surface. But how can your prospects possibly find you if you don't put up a marker to show them where you are and - most importantly - why they should use you.

You may think you've got a marker up because of all the money you're pouring into advertising. But if the message you're spending money on looks just the same as the message that all other real estate agents are using, you really haven't put up a marker at all. All that you and the other agents in your town have down is raised the water level.

Are you the #1 agent in your town, your company, your state or province? Well, take it from a customer (and I've asked the same question of hundreds of customers) - So what . . . And what this really means is, "So - what does this mean for me? What's in it for me?"

What's in it For Me?

Try to take a step back and look through a customer's eyes. Every agent in your local paper is #1 for something. Don't fool yourself into thinking that your prospects will take the time and energy to analyze all these #1 claims to figure out which one means the most. Believe me - they won't bother. And why should they? You're supposed to be telling them why they should do business with you - what's in it for them.

"Enough about you . . . Let's hear about me . . ." - Cynthia Heimel

7 Things You Should NEVER Do in Your Advertising

1. Focus on the agent, not the customer
2. Make vague and unsubstantiated claims
3. Assume that because the prospect knows who you are, they will call you. (i.e. "I just need to get my face out there") This is a mistake.
4. No benefits
5. Top Producer claim. Saying "I'm #1" or "Top Producer" or "We're the Biggest" or "We're the Best" . . . Who Cares!! These statements in and of themselves are meaningless to the average consumer
6. No Direct Response mechanism
7. Use of corny slogans or gimmicks (buying or selling a house is serious business to your prospects - they are looking to hire a professional, not a comedian.) This is a major problem in the industry, but it's a major opportunity for you

Accept the fact that most of your competitors have NO CLUE about how to market their listings or their services, and then challenge yourself to come up with a unique selling proposition that is truly unique.

How to Create A Compelling Usp

Now that we've talked about what you should NOT do in your advertising, I'm going to explain to you what you SHOULD do.

Your USP tells the world who you are and specifically what you do. It articulates clearly and concisely what benefit (or benefits) a prospect will derive from doing business with you. It answers the question:

"Why should I do business with you above all other options, including doing nothing or whatever I'm doing now?"
- Dan Kennedy

Your USP is quite basically the essence of your entire business concept; that unique advantage that distinguishes your business from all your competitors. The issues and questions you must address to determine what your unique advantage is are as follows:

1. Determine what your customers want
2. Find out which of these needs you can fill
3. Find a way to clearly state to your customers that you are the source to fill those needs - this is your USP

6 Criteria Your USP Must Incorporate

Here are some general rules of thumb to keep in mind when creating your USP:

1. **Be Unique . . .** Offer something that is truly different
2. **Be Specific . . .** It's always better to be very precise and specific. The more precise and exact a statement is, the more believable it becomes. People generally won't challenge - or even doubt - precise numbers because they assume that this precision was calculated by some kind of reliable mathematical or statistical method. Instead of naturally rounding off your statistics and saying that your homes sell for 2% more than the real estate board average, be precise and say they sell for 2.36% more.
3. **Be Relevant . . .** This means that you have to offer a benefit that means something to your prospect. You have to connect with them at some deeply felt level.

4. **Be Believable** . . . Don't offer something that is so hard to swallow that you fail to be taken seriously
5. **Be Focused** . . . Don't try to be all things to all people. But equally, don't target your message to too small a group (you have to be able to earn a sustainable income), and don't forget to keep your eye on the future (your USP may have to evolve with changes in the market)
6. **Be Concise** . . . You do NOT want a paragraph of copy. Instead, you want a single - easy to understand - thought. You must articulate - in a few words - the precise advantage you have over your competition

3 Key USP Platforms

Your USP tells your prospects clearly, concisely and specifically what benefits they will derive by working with you that they couldn't get anywhere else. I developed a number of highly successful USPs which I group under three main platforms:

- Unique Service USPs
- Performance Guarantee USPs
- Statistical USPs

Let me explain what each of these platforms accomplishes. As I've discussed, image advertising fails to address real customer needs, focusing instead on the agent. Regardless which platform my USP rests on, in every case I tell the prospect how they will benefit:

Unique Service USP . . . Shows prospects how my unique and innovative consumer programs will make buying or selling a home easier, faster or more fun, and get them superior results

Example:

- View 6 Homes in One Afternoon With My Sunday Tour of Homes
- How to Get the Information on Homes You Want Without Having to Talk With an Agent
- How to Get Advance Notice of Hot New Listings That Match Your Criteria

Performance Guarantee USP . . . Shows prospects how I go far beyond empty boasts and promises. I set myself apart from my competition by making myself accountable for the powerful guarantees I give to my clients

Example:

- Your Home Sold in Under 120 Days or I Buy It
- Move Up to Any One of My Listings and I'll Buy Your Home for Cash
- Your Home Sold in Under 60 Days or I'll Sell it for FREE
- Your Home Sold in Under 60 Days or I'll Pay You $1,000 Cash
- Your Home Sold for 100% of Market Value or I'll Pay You the Difference
- $5,000 Savings on Your Home Purchase Guaranteed or I'll Pay You $1,000

Statistical USP . . . Shows prospects specific proof (using objective, independent statistics) that my system will sell their home faster and for more money

Example:

- Your Home Will Sell for an Average $3,000 More (with graphs to back this up - my results vs. the Real Estate Board)
- Your Home Sold in 1/3 Less Time (with graphs to back this up - my results vs. the Real Estate Board)
- Your Home is 2.68 Times MORE Likely to Sell (again, demonstrates this with graphs based on Real Estate Board statistics)

It is the Performance Guarantee USPs that are most "shocking". They elicited the strongest emotions and reactions on behalf of my prospects: "How can he do that?" they would say.

Test these different USPs in different (but parallel) markets or within different time periods which are far enough apart. Find out which of these Performance USPs works best for you and then "own" it - put it on everything. These USPs will not only elicit strong response on the part of your prospects, they'll also be daunting to other agents in your marketplace. Even though any one of these USPs is easy and non-risky to execute (anyone could run them easily in their market), they will seem risky to other agents who won't even try to duplicate your strong claim.

I coach agents to run the Unique Service USPs and Statistical USPs to give backbone, substance and credibility to my "jaw dropping" Performance Guarantee USPs.

With my Unique Service USPs, I show prospects exactly how I can make, and be accountable for, my superior performance guarantees. I showcase the details and benefits of my innovative consumer programs that were founded on real customer research and developed to address real customer needs.

With my Statistical USPs, I show them real and verifiable results that prove not only how I can put my money where my mouth is (with my Performance Guarantee USPs), but also can give them multiple specific case studies of my superior system in action.

When I ran these ads in my own marketplace, I did this in two ways: via statistics and via testimonials. The statistics ads give very specific proof about what kind of service and results they can expect from me. One of the biggest mistakes I see most agents make is that their claims are completely void of any kind of proof. Most advertisers (realtors included) make claims, but very few back up any of these claims with proof.

Testimonials offer proof. Testimonials very powerfully put my USP in the mouths of other buyers or sellers who are just like them: Real Results from Real People. I ran a new testimonial every week. You should do the same.

IMPORTANT NOTE: I did NOT leave these testimonials to chance. One of my assistants (who was trained in Direct Response Marketing) interviewed my clients after the transaction was complete, drafted a testimonial based on both this interview and the stats of the sale (or purchase), and then got the client to sign off on it. Why did I do this? I did it because most testimonials I see are wimpy and non-specific. A testimonial is only valuable if it is specific and "meaty". Compare these two statements:

The Typical, Wimpy, Non-Specific,
Non-Compelling Testimonial Most Agents Use:

"Craig was great to us.
I'd really like to thank Craig for selling our house.
It was a really good experience."

VS.

The Kind of Powerful, Meaty, Highly Specific,
Highly Motivating Testimonial I Secured:

"Craig sold our Newmarket home for 98.8% of
our Asking Price in Just 9 Days!"

Which testimonial do you think would have a greater impact on a prospect? Clearly the latter. Just like your USP, your testimonials should make a strong, compelling and specific claim that causes your prospects to pay attention.

Chapter 4
Direct Response
Lead Generation

by Craig Proctor

How Highly Profitable Real Estate Sales Teams Get Business: Direct Response Lead Generation

BACKGROUND

One of the main reasons many real estate agents have such a tough time balancing their job and their life is because they're so busy working in their business as technicians that they fail to look at their business and understand what it takes to get out of the rut they're in.

If you asked the typical agent what they do for a living, they'd probably answer that they sell houses. But is this really what you do? How much of your time is actually spent "selling houses"? The fact of the matter is that there are hundreds of other tasks to perform first before you ever even get near the point of negotiating the sale of a house.

To show you what I mean, let's look at the way a typical agent spends their time. I think you'll all agree that there are really four stages in the real estate process:

- You have to **FIND** prospects

- You have to **CONVERT** these prospects into clients
- You have to provide exceptional **SERVICE** so that they become happy lifelong clients (this is the "selling houses" part of your job, but even at this stage, you're engaged in many other activities to make the actual sale happen)
- You have to **LEVERAGE** this one customer's satisfaction so they will give you their repeat business and **REFER** you to others

Within each of these four main stages, there are many, many little details that must be attended to if the total job is to get done (e.g. banging in signs, cutting keys, attaching lock boxes, writing and placing house ads, following up with prospects, providing feedback to your clients on showings etc. etc. etc.).

The fact of the matter is, there's far more to your job as real estate agent than most agents really admit to themselves. If you're like most agents, you'll tell yourself that your real job is selling houses, and these other little things are not really your job, they're just aggravating, time-consuming little details you have to attend to in order to get to the point of doing your real job.

I know I used to feel this way. How many times did I say to myself, "I just have to push away all these little details -- sweep them all away, get them all done -- and then I can work on what's really important to make my business take off."

Well, I'm sure you know how that story goes. These things never get "all done" do they? The fact is, all of these time-consuming little details are part of your job whether you like it or not, because if you don't do these parts of the job . . . well, quite simply, you won't have a job.

The most important of these tasks is finding and converting prospects, because if you don't do what it takes to find and convert prospects, you won't ever get a chance to service a client by helping them to sell their home. You can be the most ethical, hard-working real estate agent in your town with the most experience and knowledge, but if you don't have any customers, you'll starve.

The primary reason most agents fail is NOT because they're not good at the technical aspects of their business (most are), but rather because they're not good at finding prospects. Once we have a prospect, most of us are capable of doing a good job, but because our clients move infrequently (once you sell their home or help them buy a home, they don't need you anymore until they decide to move again in 5-7 years), we need a lot of customers to make the business work for us. So a very big part of our job as real estate agents is ensuring there's always a new client to service.

The other problem, of course, is that because an inordinate amount of time is usually spent trying to find this new supply of prospects, many agents don't do a very good job at servicing the few clients they do get. After all, there are only so many hours in a day. It's tough to fit everything in.

As a result, something suffers:

- You'll either have very happy clients but not many of them (because you focused on helping your clients but not at getting new clients in the door), or
- You'll have many less-than-satisfied clients who feel you did only a passable job (because you spent your time prospecting for new clients and not on helping the clients you already have.)

It's a Catch-22. In the first situation, these clients will probably use you again when it's time for them to move, but you'll have to wait 5-7 years for this to happen. In the second situation, you'll have to wait till hell freezes over before these disgruntled clients would ever use you again. **This is the vicious circle most agents find themselves in, and it's a problem effective marketing can solve, if you understand what you're doing.**

Now, in reality, none of you is oblivious to the fact that "finding" clients is a big job. We even have a term for this job -- it's called "prospecting". The difference between me and most agents is that most agents approach this task with dread, wanting to sweep it under the carpet. Ironically, however, it's a task that consumes most agents (the average agent spends approximately 85% of their time on prospecting). When I discovered this reality for myself, I made a point of taking a major step back to look at the big picture and, realizing that this part of the job wouldn't (and couldn't) go away, I decided to find a better way to go about it. And the better way to go about it is "effective marketing".

I use the qualifier "effective" when describing marketing because many of you are not strangers to the marketing process, but few agents know enough about marketing to make it work effectively for them. Let me explain.

The two most common Old School strategies that agents employ in their effort to find prospects are:

- cold calling / grunt prospecting, and
- image advertising (i.e. what the typical agent mistakes for marketing)

Because so many agents flounder back and forth between these two steps, 80% of new agents fail within their first year. They get locked inside a fatal cycle that ends up destroying their chances of success:

- the cold calling bleeds them emotionally, and
- the image advertising bleeds them financially

You see, most agents start off with traditional prospecting (just like I did); some venture into image advertising (just like I did), and then fall back to prospecting again when they decide that "marketing doesn't work." Let's understand this cycle.

Why Image Advertising Doesn't Work

When the typical agent has it up to here with prospecting, they usually throw their hands up in the air and moan about there having to be a better way. It's at this point that many agents decide that "marketing" is the "better way" to acquire new prospects. That's certainly what I thought when I reached a level of frustration and exhaustion that was too hard to bear. Marketing made sense to me. With marketing, I reasoned, I could reach my target market far more efficiently. Imagine how many prospects will read my advertising and call me to do business.

Well, I was only half right. I was correct that marketing was an efficient way of reaching a defined target of people, but because at that point I knew nothing about what made effective advertising, HARDLY ANYONE CALLED ME. You see, **the kind of advertising I engaged in made all sorts of boasts about me, but it really offered no benefits of interest to prospects.**

The advertising I did was the same kind of ineffective advertising most agents do: Image Advertising (or, more specifically, Self-Image Advertising.) Basically what these ads said was, "Here I am. There's no one like me. Aren't I great!" In other words, I talked on and on about me, me, me without giving prospects any reasons or benefits to call me over all the other agents who were saying exactly the same empty things. **The first ads I ran certainly didn't get the phone to ring for me.** You may have had a similar experience.

So what happens now? Well, for most, instead of trying to understand WHY their marketing efforts didn't work (and ultimately realizing that they've been talking to the wrong person - i.e. they've been talking to and about themselves rather than to and about their prospects), they either get out of the business, or take a fatal step BACK to prospecting. Why? "Well," they reason, "I'm getting nowhere with my marketing and it's costing me a fortune. I can't afford to keep this up." [The fatal assumption is that marketing doesn't work.] "As nauseating as prospecting is, at least it gets me one or two leads per hundred calls, and it doesn't cost me anything."

Have you heard yourself say the same thing? Well, the fact of the matter is, marketing IS the better way, but NOT if you do it the way most agents do it.

You see, the agent's self-interest is just as apparent in this image advertising as it is in his or her prospecting efforts. Basically, what you're saying to the prospect in either case is, "Hi, I'm great. Please hire me and give me your money. "You haven't answered WHY they should do this. You haven't shown them what you will do for them. In fact, you've given them NO reasons or benefits at all to use you. Instead, you've just put an image of yourself in front of them and assumed that if they know WHO you are they will call you.

Well, **it simply doesn't work this way. I learned the hard and expensive way that just because prospects know who you are, doesn't mean they'll call you.**

Instead of abandoning marketing, your challenge is to start learning about and running EFFECTIVE marketing that:

- talks to and **about your prospects**
- gives prospects **real benefits**
- gives prospects a **non-threatening way to get more information**, and
- gives prospects **compelling reasons** to contact you to get it

You see, you can't make prospects contact you. Prospects won't contact you just because you want them to. They won't contact you just because they are aware that you exist. They will only contact you if it will benefit them in some way to do so. All of us, including your prospects, have the same radio station playing in our heads: WIFM (What's in it for me). To be effective with your marketing, you must get inside your prospect's head and figure out what they want to hear - and then play it for them. If someone's a rock 'n roll fan, you'll never be able to convince them to listen to a country station. If you want them to listen to you, you better play rock.

**The Purpose of Your Marketing is NOT to Promote Yourself,
But Rather to Attract Your Prospects . . .
. . . This is a BIG Difference**

Most agents think the purpose of marketing is to promote themselves, but this isn't true. The purpose of your marketing is to ATTRACT prospects. In other words, they WON'T call you just because they are aware that you exist. They will ONLY call you if they feel it will benefit THEM to do so. So the ONLY reason you should run an ad is to get prospects to call you because, as I said before, you can be the most ethical, hard-working real estate agent in your town with the most experience and knowledge, but if you don't have any customers, you'll starve.

Some realtors still challenge me over the Image Advertising issue by saying, "Hey Craig, how come big companies like Coca Cola and Nike spend millions on image ads. How can these big companies be wrong?"

Well, they're not wrong . . . for the kind of products they sell, but that doesn't mean the kind of advertising they do would be right for real estate. Consider the following four important points that illustrate some major differences between their business and ours:

1. **Look closely to see if the advertising done by these companies is really image advertising. What you'll find is that these companies may have ads that look pretty, but they are also conveying important customer's benefits by hitting on some key emotional hot-buttons, even if their benefits are quite different in nature than the benefits you and I would offer.** Think about Coke's image of the "real thing", or the image conveyed by the beer companies. While you can't see or touch these benefits, or put them in the bank, they are, nevertheless, benefits that feed consumers in a psychological manner - they feed ego and self image and status. This is quite different from the average agent's ad which shows a picture of themselves and some vague or self-serving line such as "Great Service" or "Why Not Call Me" or "Top Producer". A runner

projects a certain "status" when he or she wears Nikes. The same mind set doesn't factor into the choice of real estate agent. It's highly unlikely that a homeowner would feel elevated in status simply by using one real estate agent over another. The services we as real estate agents market, and the products these big companies market, are worlds apart. It is, therefore, meaningless to try to compare our methods of advertising.

2. **These companies have pots more money than you or I do.** Corporate pockets are deep and can afford the luxury of running ads that will have a long-term (vs. immediate) impact, and running ads they can't really measure. You and I can't afford to do this in the same free-wheeling manner. They have major sales forces and promotion houses, mega marketing departments and consumer research budgets. If something major doesn't work, they have lots of padding that can insulate them from any major damage. If you or I fail at our marketing attempts or waste money on a campaign we're not measuring and making accountable, there are no deep pockets or corporate synergies to bail us out. ALL of our marketing efforts (whether USP or Classified or Editorial-Style Direct Response) must be hard-hitting, direct and measurable. If something isn't working, we need to know about it right away so we can change it to make it work. Failure to make our marketing dollars work efficiently could mean the difference between success or failure for you or I.

3. **These companies have a vast market area; their products are everywhere.** In contrast, most real estate agents work within a very specific geographic area which might encompass a city or two. Our target market is much smaller and much more defined.

4. **They have a much shorter re-purchase cycle than you or I.** You see, Real Estate is a very different business than soft drinks, running shoes or beer. Consumers might buy 100 cokes or more a year. They may own several pairs of sneakers. For us in real estate, it's completely different. The average consumer will only move once every five to seven years, and if we don't find them early in the process, another agent will.

What this suggests is that in addition to finding those who are ready to act right now (and may already have formed a relationship with another agent), we ALSO have to find people early in the homeselling process so we can fill the pipeline. There's a sense of urgency to our business because people are in and out of the market very quickly -- i.e. they may take 3-12 months to actually sell their home or make a purchase, but once this is accomplished, they're out of the market for several years. This is quite unlike the purchase of lower ticket items such as food or clothing, for example, where the decision making process is short but there are many repeat purchases during a year.

In fact, the purchase process for real estate is quite different than the purchase process for the highly visible products we see around us -- not in terms of the content or order of the stages followed, but in terms of the length of time between and during the stages. It's important to talk about purchase process because it underlies the highly effective 3-pronged marketing approach I've developed for my real estate business. We'll discuss this shortly. But first, I want to make sure you're very clear about the fundamental difference between the kind of (ineffective) advertising most agents do, and the highly effective advertising I developed for my system. **In simplest terms, my advertising uses the prospects' needs (rather than the agent's ego) as a springboard to the message conveyed.** Let me explain to you in another way why this major shift in focus is so critical.

Why You Must Listen To Your Prospects (The Importance of Tuning In To WIFM)

Fishing makes an excellent analogy to the marketing process. When you go fishing, your objective is to end up with a lot of fish in your boat at the end of the day. But how do you get a fish into your boat?

Well, **when you spend your time cold-calling and door-knocking, it's like standing in the water and trying to snatch fish out with your bare hands.** Often, you're not even sure there are fish to be found here, but you stand there in desperation, thrashing about at anything that moves, **knowing that if you don't find something, you'll starve.**

Even if you chance upon a prime fishing ground, your results (i.e. fish in the boat) won't dramatically improve. You may actually see them swimming around you, and this may make you feel hopeful. "Surely I can catch some of these," you reason. "There are so many of them." Soon enough, however, you find that this doesn't really improve your odds. The fact is, fishing with your bare hands is highly ineffective. If you're lucky enough to catch one and hold onto it, you've undoubtedly had a thousand more slip through your fingers, or evade your grasp altogether. **Rejection**

is a way of life for someone who fishes with their hands (or who cold-call prospects in real estate.)

So then you get the bright idea to try fishing with a pole. All you have to do is throw out your line and the fish will bite. Right? It looks pretty easy. This is what most agents think when they decide to abandon cold calling and try marketing. All you have to do is show your face and prospects will come flocking to you. Right?

Well, back to our fishing analogy and let's see what actually happens. The first time you try pole fishing, you go out and spend a lot of money on some fancy lures. You buy the ones that are big and colorful and beautiful. You feel in your heart that the more money you spend, and the fancier the lure is, the more fish you'll catch. "If they see you, they will come," you think. How can you possibly fail? Well, if you've ever fished, you've undoubtedly known the frustration of sitting in your boat, with your line in the water dangling your fancy, expensive lure, and watching the fish swimming around and around and IGNORING your lure!

"How can this be?" you whine. "Look at how much money I spent! Look at how pretty that lure is? How could the fish possibly miss it! What's wrong with those fish anyway? Don't they know this is the best lure money can buy? It's crafted of the best metal and painted with the best paints. It's rated #1 by the fishing association for heaven's sake. Surely that's got to impress the fish."

But it doesn't seem to attract the fish, does it? In fact, after all the money you've spent on fancy lures and spiffy poles, at the end of the day, there aren't really very many more fish in the boat than when you used the caveman method of snatching with your bare hands.

It Never Occurs to Most to Ask the CRITICAL Question: "What Do the Fish Want?"

So what most do at this point is go back to the caveman method. It's not very effective either, but at least it doesn't cost as much. It never occurs to them to ask the question, "What do the fish want? What would make the fish want to bite the lure at the end of my line?" This is a fatal mistake, because without asking this critical question, there's only one place to go . . . backwards.

Most real estate agents are also victims to this very narrow mind set. Instead of realizing that their fancy advertising is ineffective, because it's not saying anything of interest to the prospect, they quickly conclude that marketing itself is over-rated and ineffective.

Even Fish Are Listening to WIFM

If the fisherman had done some research and discovered that the kind of fish he or she was after craved earthworms, and if he or she had put a wriggling earth worm on the end of a hook (even a very simple and inexpensive hook), what do you think would have happened? Right, the fish would have bitten the hook because it wanted the earthworm.

You see, the reason the fish didn't bite the expensive, beautiful lure is because those fish couldn't care less how expensive or beautiful a lure is, it will only bite a lure if there's something on it that it wants (even fish are listening to WIFM.)

So what does that mean for you and your marketing efforts?

Well, follow the analogy through to something closer to real estate but this time put yourself in the shoes of the prospect. Let's take the process of buying a car. When you go to buy a car, do you care that the salesperson at your local car dealership is the top salesperson in your town or country or world? Do you care that this car salesman plays the guitar or loves dogs or has a nice smile? Does the dealerships slogan, "We Care" do anything for you? Or are you more interested in getting the best car for your money? Clearly it's the latter.

Well, your prospects are no different than car shoppers or fish. None of them really cares too much about you, instead they care about themselves. The fact is, my marketing is highly effective because I make it my business to understand what my prospects want. I know how to craft marketing that, like that little worm on the end of a hook, compels my prospects to bite, and this is what I teach agents.

While all good marketing starts from the same premise (i.e. offering prospects an easy way to get something they want), there are many different proven methods that I share with agents in my training programs. In direct contrast with the Self-Image advertising that some agents do, and as shocking as this may seem to you, much of the marketing I teach doesn't even mention your name (well, your name is there for legal reasons, but it's small and unprominent). But all of it ultimately accomplishes the same goal - to generate a steady stream of motivated prospects who are eager to use you to buy or sell a home.

This kind of advertising is called EMOTIONAL DIRECT RESPONSE MARKETING, and I'll explain to you shortly the 3 Pronged Marketing

Approach I teach which is based on the principles of emotional direct response. First, let's look at the issue of purchase process.

Purchasing Is A Process Not An Event

Purchasing a home is a process, NOT an event. People generally don't wake up one morning, without any preamble, and go buy or sell a house. Instead, the decision to buy and sell an item as large as a home takes place over time.

In fact, purchasing anything -- even a chocolate bar -- is a process and not an event. While the length of the process, and the thought that goes into each stage of the process, may differ depending on the kind of product you're purchasing, the stages themselves are pretty universal:

1. You **discover that you have a need** (e.g. your present living arrangements are inadequate)
2. You **decide to do something about that need** (e.g. you decide to sell and/or buy a home)
3. You **consider your options** (e.g. sell your home yourself or use an agent; buy a brand new home or buy a resale, etc.)
4. You **choose an option** (e.g. choose agent John Doe to help buy a resale)

What implications does this have on you as a real estate agent? Well, as discussed above, like it or not, a significant part of your job in real estate is to find customers. And knowing that at any given point in time there are prospects at different stages in the purchase process described above, if you want to have a steady stream of prospects calling you to do business, you will need to:

1. Make sure you have a way of attracting those prospects who are ready to make a move right NOW (ready-to-act buyers and sellers)
2. Make sure you have a way of identifying those prospects who will be ready to make a move in the near future (3-12 months) and be able to engage them in a follow-up process before they form a relationship with another agent
3. Make sure all area prospects have top-of-mind-consciousness of the unique and special way you can help them with their home moving needs so when they start to think about moving, they will consider you as an option

The three types of advertising which are most responsible for doing these three important jobs in my system are: Classified Ads, Editorial-Style Advertising and USP Advertising. I will talk about Emotional Direct Response Advertising, and my specific 3-Pronged Marketing Approach next.

Emotional Direct Response Advertising: My 3-Pronged Approach

Emotional Direct Response Marketing is as UNLIKE Image Advertising as it is from Prospecting. **With Emotional Direct Response Marketing, you offer people what they are dying to know, and then they contact you to get it.** In other words, in direct contrast to Prospecting and Image Advertising, with Emotional Direct Response Marketing, **your focus is NOT ON YOU, but rather ON YOUR PROSPECTS' NEEDS**, so that your prospect is motivated (not manipulated) into action on their own volition.

When you turn the tables on the process in this manner, astonishingly, you **won't have to cold-call prospects ever again**, because prospects will call you. It's that simple. I call this Reverse Prospecting, and the best part is, it can happen AUTOMATICALLY.

Every single ad in my system is crafted to create this reverse prospecting effect. At the back of my mind at all times when developing my marketing is the question, "Will this compel qualified prospects to do something they are naturally averse to doing?" (i.e. contact a real estate agent.) Is my offer so in tune with their needs -- so motivating -- that they will take the step to contact me?

And remember, it doesn't matter what I think. I may develop an ad that I think will be a jackpot, but if it doesn't compel prospects to respond, it wasn't a good ad. The only vote that counts is the customer's. Driving your customers to your website or hotline makes this testing process incredibly easy. I monitored the results of my ads every day to understand what was working and what wasn't -- what I should do more of and what I should change. I hope all of you are using this invaluable tool in your business

I have spent many years and thousands of dollars testing ads to understand what works and why. As mentioned, as a result of this testing, I teach three key types of advertising:

- USP advertising
- Editorial Style advertising
- Classified advertising

While each of these three types is engineered toward the same ultimate goal (i.e. to get prospects to contact you), each type of advertising achieves this end in a different way. When creating ads in any of these three categories, I ensure that I follow 6 basic principles of emotional direct response advertising:

1. Understand what **benefits** your prospect wants and offer them in your ad
2. Communicate these benefits in an attention-grabbing, **compelling** and motivating manner
3. Make an offer that has **universal appeal** to your defined target (i.e. it is specific enough to attract your prospects, but not so specific that it eliminates them)
4. Make a **soft offer** that is non-threatening for prospects to respond to (e.g. "free information" is a soft offer because you're not trying to "sell" anything to the prospect. Prospects don't feel that they will be pressured into any purchase or threatened by any sales pitch. Instead, they can get this information in the privacy and comfort of their own home and make any decisions without a hovering agent looking over their shoulder. Information is a terrific offer because it's inexpensive to produce but has a high perceived value.)
5. Make it **easy and non-threatening** for your prospects to get further information and to leave their name and address to get this information
6. Incorporate mechanisms (i.e. ID#) which make your ads **trackable and testable**

The psychology behind how and why each of the 3-prongs of my marketing arsenal works is both fascinating and important for you to understand. First I'll review my S-O-L-D formula which gives you a blueprint for effective emotional direct response advertising, and then I'll look briefly at each of the 3 advertising prongs.

The S-O-L-D Formula For Effective Emotional Direct Response Advertising

You don't need a writing or advertising degree to be good at creating these ads. All you have to do is follow the formula, and the formula is:

S-O-L-D

I created this acronym because it parallels the ultimate result you're looking for your day-to-day business. The simple measure of success or failure in your work selling houses is whether you manage to get a SOLD sign put up. If you do, you were successful. If this doesn't happen, you failed.

Well, it's the same with your advertising. The formula for success is in these four letters: S-O-L-D.

S top them in their tracks (The Headline)

O perate on their self-interest and desires (Make it compelling)

L ure them with a story about something they want (Your offer)

D eliver them to your door (Call to Action)

Let's understand this step-by-step.

STOP THEM IN THEIR TRACKS *(The Headline)*

How I Compel Hundreds of Ready-to-Act Buyers and Sellers to Call Me and How You Can Do the Same

The first thing prospects see is your headline. Your headline is the ad for the ad. Your headline must **STOP** prospects in their tracks. Remember, you've only got about 2 seconds to accomplish this, less time than it took you to read this sentence. If you fail to do this, your prospect will merely turn the page, and it will be just as if your ad wasn't there at all. Running an ad without a headline is like going fishing without a lure. In fact, according to advertising guru David Ogilvy, "on average, **five times as many people read headlines as read the body copy.**" Research proves that **80-90% of the success of any ad is a direct result of how well the headline gets attention.**

Your headline must grab your prospect by the throat. It must be selective, precise, motivating, attention getting, big picture, full of benefits. You'll probably want to write 10 or so headlines first before you decide which one to use.

There are 4 qualities that good headlines may possess. There are:

1. Self Interest
2. News
3. Curiosity
4. Quick, Easy Way

OPERATE ON THEIR SELF-INTEREST AND DESIRES
(Make it Compelling)

If you managed to sneak your headline past their advertising radar in your 2 second window, you've got 5 seconds more to keep it up. Your headline is simply the door opener. <u>Make it specifically and abundantly clear that you're talking about something that will directly benefit prospects in some way. Appeal to their self-interest, wants and desires.</u>

And remember, people don't buy *products*, they buy *advantages*. They don't listen to *selling* points they listen to *buying* points. They don't care about *features*, they care about *benefits*. So talk about these benefits.

Let me repeat this important point:

People Buy *Benefits*, NOT *Features*

So instead of saying "Down filled", say "Twice the warmth at half the weight". Instead of saying "Gas Shock Absorbers", say "Smoother Ride". Instead of saying "Top Producer" say "Sell Faster and for More Money".

Remember, the only things we really need in life are air, water, food and sleep. We don't need a new car or home or vacation, but we may want these things passionately.

Logic has nothing to do with it. **Emotion has everything to do with it.**

<u>Deepen their interest. Make it impossible for them to pass you by. Spell out their specific wants and then explain in simple, factual language how your product or service fills those needs.</u>

LURE THEM WITH A STORY ABOUT SOMETHING THEY WANT *(Your Offer)*

Always remember that **you're only talking to one person** and one person only. <u>The person reading your ad</u>.

After the first 7 seconds, your job is now to earn their continued attention. Don't be afraid of making your ad too long. Make it as long as it needs to be - but no longer. People will read what interests them, so tell a complete and interesting story. But don't pad it unnecessarily. Remember . . .

People Will Not Allow
You to Bore Them
Woo Them. Romance Them. Get Them to
See Themselves in Your Copy.

Talk to them as if they were your friend. Your close friend. You should view your ad as a conversation - a very personal conversation - with this close friend. By the end of this conversation, this person should be on your side because . . .

You Should Have Connected with Them

You should have **spoken to their heart** in deep enough terms that they will want what you have to offer. (And remember, in real estate it's a multi-step process. One ad probably won't make them hire you, but it should make them call you for the information - the soft, non-threatening offer - you've made them).

Make sure you:

- <u>**State what you're offering early**</u> on in the copy
- <u>**Make it easy for skimmers**</u> to get the essence of your story by using effective heads and subheads
- <u>**Use bullets, underlining and bold type**</u> to make it easier to navigate

<u>NEVER assume knowledge</u>. You know your business inside-out, but your prospects don't. **ALWAYS state the obvious**.

Deliver them to do your door *(Call to Action)*

Ask them to do something. **Demand action**. And make it easy for them to comply. Ask them to pick up the phone and call you for a FREE special report on the thing their heart desires. Give them an 800#. Tell them they don't have to talk with anybody. Tell them it will be delivered to their door, with no obligation, free of charge. And / or, tell them they can get this information online by giving them a benefit-rich domain name.

In other words, state as precisely and clearly as possible what it is you want them to do (you'll find that people will do what you tell them to do if you make it easy). Motivate them into action. Create a sense of urgency with a special incentive or a bonus. Tell them exactly what steps to take: Order Today . . ., Respond By . . ., Send For Your Free . . ., Pick Up the Phone and Call Immediately . . .

Classified Ads

I've talked to you about the value of making an information offer to your prospects. Now, in actual fact, most of you are probably making some kind of "information" offer to your prospects that falls under the realm of Direct Response advertising without even knowing it.

You see, direct response advertising as an art form is far from new. Real estate agents have been using direct response advertising for 100 years. After all, what else is a classified house ad but a direct response ad? When you run an ad for one of your listings, you don't really expect the prospect who calls in to buy the house in the ad, do you.

One of the biggest mistakes many agents make is trying to sell the house in the ad when this is almost an impossible goal.) 99% of the time, you don't sell the house you advertised, but you DO get prospects to raise their hands, don't you?

Almost all real estate agents run classified house ads, but few realize what a powerful tool a classified ad can be when it's crafted properly. The failure in the real estate industry is not recognizing that some kinds of ads work better than others. The problem with running traditional house ads is that if none of your listings interests Mr. or Mrs. Homeseller, they won't call you. It's hit and miss. That's why your offer has to have a more universal appeal to this highly targeted group of consumers.

The fact of the matter is, **classified ads are the most effective (and least expensive) way I know of to find NOW business.** With my classified ads, you're able to attract prospects who have already gone through steps 1 and 2 of the purchase process (i.e. they've discovered their need and decided to do something about it), and are now considering their options in order to make a choice

Editorial-style ads are crafted to fly under your prospects' advertising radar in order to attract future business. Most of the prospects you attract with your editorial-style ads will be thinking about moving and looking for information about moving. Now, of course, a classified ad is very different. To begin with, most of these prospects have already made the decision that they are moving soon, and they are reading the classified ads to "shop" for a home (as mentioned earlier, they have already taken the first two steps of the purchase process and are now at the point of considering their options in order to make a choice.)

As a general rule, then, these prospects are further along in the thought process about moving, and are now in the doing stage. They're starting to carry out their plan. (I said as a "general rule", because certainly some of the prospects reading the classifieds are also longer term prospects - renters who perhaps want to buy a home, but don't think they can afford one yet. They scan the classifieds with their eye and their dreams on the future. This is an important point I dig into and train agents to understand and leverage.

While the majority of the prospects reading the classifieds will be buyers, many of these buyers will also have homes to sell. I teach agents how to attract BOTH buyers and sellers with this medium. But an important point to make here is that it is much easier to attract buyers than it is to attract sellers, and there are two reasons for this:

1.   If people have a home to sell, in most cases they will want to scout out what's available for purchase before they take the major step of listing their home for sale. Therefore, advertising that attracts buyers is a smart way of finding prospects who may also be sellers.
2.   Most agents grow up in this industry thinking that listings are the most important part of the business, and people know that real estate agents are hungry for listings. As a result, if they respond to an ad as a seller, they know that they'll be hounded by dozens of agents all looking for their business.

In other words, it's much easier to get prospects to respond as a buyer than as a seller.

Your Classified Ads Must Fly INTO Their Advertising Radar

As mentioned, another major difference between classified ads and editorial-style ads is that you won't have to take any steps to fly under the prospect's advertising radar with your classified ads, because these prospects already know they are reading advertisements (you'll find more information about my editorial ads a little further along in this chapter). The classified section, by definition, is 100% advertisements, so rather than trying NOT to look like an ad, your focus here is to understand how to jump off a page which is filled with advertisements from agents just like you who are all trying to get the same prospects' attention. Rather than flying under their advertising radar, with your classified ads, you must instead fly straight into their line of radar and make sure you're seen.

Contrary to what you might think, the answer to how you do this has little to do with having a bigger ad, a more colorful ad, or the inclusion of a photo. In fact, it has very little to do with how your ad looks.

Editorial-Style Ads

Editorial-style ads are exactly what their name implies: i.e. they're ads which look like newspaper editorial. I teach agents to place them in the middle of other real newspaper editorial in an attempt to fly under prospects' advertising radar and catch the attention of those who are very early in the purchase process. They cost more than classified ads, but they also do a different kind of job.

The key with this type of ad is that you're filling your pipeline with FUTURE business by attracting prospects before they even really know themselves that they're really in the market - when their thoughts of buying or selling are just beginning. How do these ads do this?

Well, with these editorial style ads, you again offer your prospects something they want . . . free information . . . and this compels them to contact you.

Specifically, you make a risk-free offer to these people which offers to give them answers to the questions that are just beginning to form in their minds. But you have to be there early if you want to gain the competitive edge.

Many of them will be so early in the process that they are really just discovering that they have a need. In fact, your "editorial" may even be the piece of the puzzle which causes them to understand and articulate for the first time that they have this need. These people are sellers and buyers who have probably not yet (but will soon) formed an alliance with an agent. These are the prospects who will flow through your pipeline and may not emerge out the other end for months or even a year, but once the flow through effect starts to kick in, the amount of business that pours out the funnel is double or triple or more what it would be if you only ran classified ads. As with classified ads, editorial-style ads will not build top-of-mind consciousness for you, but they will cause prospects to call you, and you will have plenty of opportunity in your follow up process to build a relationship so they will end up choosing you to represent them.

USP Advertising

USP Ads may not seem to be as effective as classified ads and editorial-style ads at generating leads (although they can do this job too), and USP advertising is generally more expensive than these other types of advertising, but it is highly effective at generating top-of-mind consciousness and changing prospects' perceptions. This is important if you want to build a long term business, and I'll tell you why. If all you do is classified and editorial-style advertising to attract your prospects, you will always have a further job to do to convince them that they should choose you over other agents they may be talking with. With USP advertising, however, you can create meaningful top-of-mind consciousness which has some longevity in the marketplace.

Let's break that term -- "meaningful top-of-mind consciousness" -- into two parts. One part is the issue of awareness -- how aware people are that you exist.

One of the marketing gurus put it this way. If a door-to-door salesman came to your door selling computers and presented you with two brands for the same price with exactly the same features but one was an IBM and one was a brand you'd never heard of before, in most cases, everything else being equal, you would buy the IBM. Why? Because you've heard of IBM, and your neighbors and relatives and friends have heard of IBM. IBM has publicly demonstrated an expertise in the computer industry that most people believe and accept. They have a good reputation for helping people in a meaningful way with their computer problems. Even if the unknown brand is exactly the same as the IBM, odds are people will choose the IBM because there's not as much risk associated with this purchase. People don't like risk.

But awareness on its own is not nearly enough to win a prospect's business. There were plenty of other agents in my town who had a high profile, but I still did better in my marketplace than they did. Why? Because I was much more than just a well-known face to the people in my town. Instead of just creating awareness as some others did, I linked that awareness with some very powerful, compelling and meaningful points of difference or USPs. Where other agents were saying, "Why Not Give Us a Call" or "Top Producer", I told prospects that I'd buy their home. This is a big difference. A big fancy image may create top of mind consciousness, but without compelling consumer benefits attached to this consciousness, it's unlikely you'll get many calls.

Summary

To summarize, the purpose of your classified and editorial-style direct response ads is to get prospects to contact you. 80% of the business you generate from classified ads will be NOW business. This equation is reversed for editorial-style ads where 80% will represent FUTURE business.

USP advertising should also generate calls for you. Although USP ads will probably only represent 5-10% of the calls you receive on a daily basis, they also have a larger function which is to change customer perceptions about you and create meaningful and relevant top-of-mind consciousness for your services (i.e. demonstrate clearly why prospects should choose you over all other agents.) Importantly, this will impact how well you are received when you commence follow up with prospects.

When I ran an editorial style ad which offered free information about how to avoid 7 costly mistakes when selling, prospects not only raised their hands, but they also viewed me as an Information Provider and NOT a salesperson. This is a very important distinction.

When I ran a classified ad for one of my listings, I may have created some interest in my client's property, but the main reason I ran this ad was not to try to sell the house in the ad (in fact, as I teach agents, it's nearly impossible to sell the house in an ad) - the only reason I ran this ad was to get prospects to call me.

In both cases I was offering prospects information about something they wanted (e.g. tips on selling, or information about a specific property) and strategically positioning my ad to either fly under their radar (in the case of my editorial-style ads) or right in the face of their advertising radar (in the case of my classified and USP ads). In both cases I made it easy and non-threatening for them to get this information (by directing them either to my website or to my toll free hotline, and I tell them in the ad that this is where they can access the information without having to speak to a salesperson.) so that they do exactly what I want them to do which is to initiate this contact and leave their contact information.

Once they do this, you have another qualified name in your Automatic Reverse Prospecting System (ARPS) pipeline, and this is the way the system works. And the system will work if you follow the rules.

What this all means is the following. Ultimately, you should be doing all three kinds of advertising (and some of the other kinds which fall into one of more of these categories), but the speed with which you're able to incorporate all three may vary depending on your circumstances.

Classified Ads are the foundation from where most of my students' leads are generated. They are the least expensive, yet most effective way of driving prospects to your website or hotline. The versatility of classified ads is another reason why they are so effective, and why we suggest you make these the foundation of your lead generation system. Rather than only running classified ads in your local newspaper, dozens, or even hundreds of leads can be generated online from online sources such as Google Pay Per Click, Craigslist, Postlets, Kijiji and more. all of which are effective, yet inexpensive. Editorial style ads and USP ads have a role in your marketing system, but only once a foundation has been laid with the classified offers.

Chapter 5
The Lead Flow Chart

by Todd Walters

The Highly Profitable Real Estate Sales Team Lead Flow System

You should have read in previous chapters that the way you grow your real estate business is by having an over flow of it. Whether you are doing 50 transactions or 500, you must have an overflow of buyers and/or sellers in order to do more business. **More business than YOU or your present team members can handle means you have opportunity for growing your business.**

Let's assume you have some great buyer and seller lead generation systems in place. You have GOOD leads to follow up with. More than you can get to, so you have hired outside sales agents to help you handle the overflow. After some time doing this, you and your OSA's are super busy and leads begin to fall through the cracks, so you hire more OSA's, but then you realize the one thing that Craig Proctor discovered many years ago: that OSA's want appointments, not leads. You discover they have been cherry picking the easy leads while failing to follow up with the longer term prospects. Therefore costing you a lot of business.

This is why Craig created the Follow Up Call Coordinator. Later renamed "Inside Sales Agent".

I remember way back in the mid 90's getting some awesome ads from Craig called "editorial ads". These ads look like news, and ran in the general news section of the local community newspapers. They were and still are amazing lead generators for getting seller prospects.

Here is one of Craig's Editorial Ads. Notice the ad offers the prospect a FREE REPORT by calling the info line or going to a special website to get it.

EXHIBIT A: Sample Editorial Ad

27 Quick and Easy Fix Ups to Sell Your Home Fast and for Top Dollar

Newmarket - A new report has just been released which reveals 7 costly mistakes that most homeowners make when selling their home, and a 9 Step System that can help you sell your home fast and for the most amount of money.

This industry report shows clearly how the traditional ways of selling homes have become increasingly less and less effective in today's market. The fact of the matter is that fully three quarters of homesellers don't get what they want for their homes and become disillusioned and - worse - financially disadvantaged when they put their homes on the market.

As this report uncovers, most homesellers make 7 deadly mistakes that cost them literally thousands of dollars. The good news is that each and every one of these mistakes is entirely preventable. In answer to this issue, industry insiders have prepared a free special report entitled "The 9 Step System to Get Your Home Sold Fast and For Top Dollar".

To order a FREE Special Report, visit www.UniqueDomainName.com or to hear a brief recorded message about how to order your FREE copy of this report call toll-free 1-800-000-0000 and enter 1000. You can call any time, 24 hours a day, 7 days a week.

Get your free special report NOW to find out how you can get the most money for your home.

This report is courtesy of Your Required identification. Not intended to solicit buyers or sellers currently under contract. Copyright © 2015

Anyone considering making a move who is reading through the front part of the newspaper would be stopped in their tracks upon seeing this ad. They would read it and many would follow through on the offer for the free report. And when I say many, I mean many. So many, in fact, that it created an overflow of seller prospects. This ad would get now business and it would get future business.

Yes, that means some were ready to discuss selling, others were longer term prospects. And this would prove to be a problem IF giving the leads directly to Outside Sales Agents. Again, Agents want appointments more than leads, so overall, we discovered that it was a better business practice to sort out the longer term leads and give those to ISA's and for those that were ready to buy now or sell now, those we could give directly to outside sales agents.

So let me clear this up for you. With our great lead generating systems, we got leads that were ready to act now AND we got leads that were wanting to make a move in a longer time frame. AND when our outside sales agents' plates got full, they would no longer do a good job of following up with the leads that required follow up. Because of this, Craig created the Lead Flow System.

The Lead Flow Chart (see Exhibit B below) is a good representation of how all of this worked.

Exhibit B Lead Flow Chart

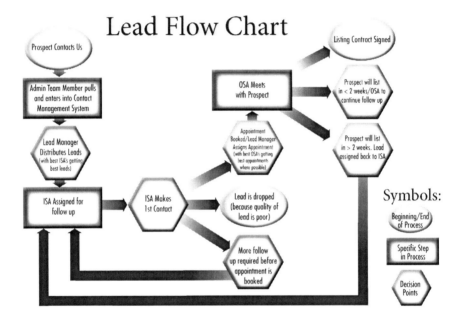

Lead Flow Chart

This system for handling the leads was/is brilliant AND is the best system for highly profitable real estate sales teams.

With that, let me walk you through this Lead Flow Chart.

Here's how it works. Firstly, the prospects contact us through our reverse marketing systems. That means with **our unique marketing and advertising,** we stop the prospects in their tracks, they raise their hand and identify themselves as a prospect. **They contact us. That's right, all of our prospects contact us; we don't do any cold-calling, door knocking or manual grunt prospecting**. All of the prospects that we generate contact us. (See the editorial ad in Exhibit A as just one example).

Now, that's the first step.

Next, our administrative team leader pulls all the leads off of our various lead capture systems and **all the data is input immediately** into our contact management system. Our leads manager then distributes the leads with **the best inside sales agents** and **the best outside sales agents** getting **the best leads. With many of the online marketing systems, the lead would come in and go straight to the Inside Sales Agent, thanks to automation.**

An inside sales agent on our team, assigned to the lead, gives the prospect a call, following up with them. That's the first point of contact. At this first point of contact, the inside sales agent determines that either more follow up is required before booking the appointment, or the lead is dropped because the quality of the lead is too low or we book an appointment. **Since we generate many ready-to-act prospect leads, getting an appointment is most likely.** We then assign the appointment to the best outside sales agent. Then, of course, the outside sales agent goes on the appointment.

After the outside sales agent reviews our Exclusive Seller or Buyer presentation with the prospect, depending on the need, they are going to sign an agreement with us, either a listing or buyer contract. The prospect may do a post-dated agreement if they are not quite ready at that time, but we will continue to follow up with them to make sure we are on-track to proceed, when the time is right.

If the prospect is more than two weeks out then they are kicked back over to our inside sales agent for follow up and the process starts all over again.

You can see from the Lead Flow Chart (Exhibit B above) how the outside sales agent on our award winning real estate sales team gets a **steady-stream of the best** and **most-motivated and qualified buyers and sellers**. They are not spending time chasing prospects around town who are not interested in talking or are not ready to move.

With this system, all of the leads are followed up with and opportunities are maximized.

Chapter 6
Steal Lesser Agents' Listings

by Todd Walters

Breakthrough Report Uncovers Evidence of a Sinister Conspiracy to Steal Lesser Agents Listings Before They Ever Even Get Them!

Inside This Chapter You Will Find . . .

When You Apply the Concept of Leverage, Your Real Estate Business Actually Becomes a Business (meaning it works without you)!

Why Direct Response Marketing is the Fastest Way to MORE Quality Buyer and Seller Leads and Some Cool Examples!

Hey – If You Can't Measure It, Don't Do It!

And . . . MORE Lessons Learned from a Billion Dollar Agent

WARNING: These agents are out to steal your business, and you don't even know it . . .

So what in the world am I talking about, who are the thieves? Well, it would be agents like ME! I will take your business if you don't watch out. Or better yet, agents like me, Craig Proctor, Marnie Bennett, Nathan Clark, Francois Mackay, Francis Lavoie, Carol Royce, Jim Bottrell and others you will hear from in the pages of this book.

Here's what's interesting, we don't even know WHO we are taking it from. Only that some poor, lesser agent out there, will never see the listing we just took.

I say lesser because they just don't really know what works, or better yet, what business they are really, really in (poor because they don't sell very many homes).

What did you get into the real estate business for? Well if you are like most agents you got into it to make more money and have more free time. Many quickly find out that you don't make much money . . . and so much for free time! 80% or more of all agents exit the business shortly after getting in. Moreover, 95% of all agents make less than $100,000 a year and 98% or so make under $250,000 a year.

I remember speaking in front of a large gathering of agents and made the statement that 95% of all real estate agents are WRONG about how to make real money in this business. I got some sneers and some silent boos, but that's only because I called some of them out. In order to move forward you must recognize where you are and understand that in order to get a different result, you have to do things differently.

So before I get to what I opened with and detail for you the warning about losing business, you don't even know you are losing, let's talk about something very important to those who want to take their business to the next level. That would be - leverage.

Leverage is the power to maximize results with the least amount of energy, time, and money. One sales trainer guru (several for that matter) advocates sitting down, picking up the phone, and cold calling prospects. That means You doing one task at that moment, that offers NO leverage. BUT, if I hired 3 telemarketers to call expireds and FSBO's – all at the same time – I have now leveraged that task, and I personally can work on something else. I am not advocating running out and hiring telemarketers to call Expireds; quite the contrary – just making a point about leverage that I knew you would understand.

How I would handle this task is actually quite different. I would most likely direct mail ALL of the expireds and FSBO's a Direct Response Marketing Sales Letter that would have a large percentage of those prospects CALL me, instead of me chasing them. A few hours of my time invested in writing and testing the sales letter and then DONE. I can send hundreds, even thousands out with a predictable result. I can even have this done while I am out fly fishing or watching my oldest daughter's softball game, or youngest daughter's tennis match.

And if I am really good, I can leverage the sales letter. My offer can address those who are ready to talk to me now to call me direct and for those that are not quite ready or skeptical, I can offer them to call an info line and hear a recorded message about the inner workings of my special offers in the sales letter, or have them visit a landing page and order a free report that details my offer – and then decide whether it's right for them.

Here is another example of leverage. When I first began generating seller leads through the killer marketing I was learning from Craig Proctor, many of the seller prospects were NOT my buddies or referrals from buddies. They had no clue who I was or what I could do for them. So my call back script was important.

Let's look at this ad example:

How to Sell Your Home Without an Agent. Free Report Reveals what you need to know to sell your home yourself and save the commission. Call 1-800-000-0000 ID 0000# (talk to no agent).

Of course this ad generated quite a number of leads, prospects wanting the report. BUT, are they expecting MY call? No. So my call back script had to acknowledge who I was and why I was calling them first.

"Hello Mr. Smith, This is Todd Walters, With Todd Walters Real Estate. I received your request for the 'Sell with No Agent Report' and we have sent that on over to you. Is that OK?"

The seller obviously says yes, that's fine – thus allowing me an opportunity to ask a few more questions and make them an offer they can't refuse. I am simply leveraging the law of reciprocity. (Incidentally, the above opening is the beginning of our Universal Follow Up Script that we teach members in our coaching programs).

BUT – remember this seller and I have NO relationship. They have agreed to let me come over after they said yes to my offer, but now I may have to work hard at selling them on listing with me. So to combat that, I would send the seller a pre-selling package called *The Ultimate Converter* as well as *The Bomb*. (*The Ultimate Converter* is an *online* preselling system we developed exclusively for our members and the *Bomb* is the *Off Line* Preselling Shock and Awe system sent ahead of any listing appointments to turn the seller into a come list me).

This allowed me to leverage the opportunity to pre-sell the seller on listing with me. This way when I showed up, they were much more likely to list with me AND at the right price AND at MY fee.

I may have gotten the listing without sending *The Ultimate Converter*, but getting my listing price and my fee – that would be more difficult without pre-selling the seller on the benefits of doing business with me, trusting me and my experience(s). And of course, if the seller does opt to interview other agents, it's unlikely they will be able to compete with me now. The value presented is just too good, even if I am 1 – 2% more. They believe that they will GET more with me, and statistics bear that out.

Direct Response Marketing is the Only Marketing If You Want to Be a Millionaire Agent!

You may not have any desire to be a 7 figure income agent. That's ok, but you still want sellers and buyers – so if Direct Response Marketing works for the TOP agents, it will work for you. We are experts of direct response marketing. One reason, among many, that we like it is because it is measurable.

Here is a simple example of direct response (emotional response) marketing

When you list two homes – you have the same for sale sign in front of both. BUT, I bet you that one house gets more calls than the other. Why is that? RIGHT, one of the homes is more desirable. Buyer drives by, house stops him is his tracks, buyer calls you to get more. The buyer's EMOTIONS took over, because the house spoke to him.

Your ads can work the same way. But most agents' ads aren't very good. They try to be all things to all people, and as Craig taught me, that will dilute your effectiveness.

I remember being faced with a dire predicament several years ago. TOO many listings that were not selling. More and more foreclosures were stealing my buyers. Buyers driving past my well-priced listings and deciding to view the foreclosure down the road, which many times was listed at a higher price. I concluded it was because the home said FORECLOSURE on the sign or somewhere.

So I invented a system called RBID to draw attention to my listings, creating a perception that my listings must be some kind of third party sell. When in fact RBID was simply a website for the property and the buyer to bid on it. A name, "RBID", did the work of emotionally stopping the buyer in his tracks and compelling action – hence direct response.

Here is a screen shot of the RBID sign that worked like Magic. The phone numbers in this sign have been changed as well as the URL, but you get the picture as an example.

The Public Notice STOPS buyers in their tracks – the RBID HOME automatically creates a 3rd party perception of sell and the offer for FREE 24Hr. Info creates a direct response. NOWHERE does it say "HEY, Call Me the Real Estate Agent so I can Sell You Something . . ." Quite the opposite. Direct Response Marketing focuses on the Prospect NOT necessarily the agent.

Measure to Gain

One of the other cool things I learned from Craig Proctor was how to measure results. This is a game-changer for your business, if you will DO IT. Most agents remain poor (below the poverty line), selling 1, 2 or 3 homes a year (not my numbers, IMS numbers, 50- 55% of all agents who sell a house, sell 1, 2 or 3 houses a year max) because they are unwilling to do things necessary to be successful. One such thing is measuring results.

To jump forward, **if you can't measure it, do not do it.** Everything in your business is measurable, if you want it to be. I will ask Platinum Members what their #1 Lead Generator is and some will tell me, "I generated 400 leads from pay per click last month . . ." My next question is, what is your number one Closing Generator? The answers to these questions reveal two important things. Is their biggest lead generator generating the best quality leads and are they redirecting resources to that which is providing their best leads. Where Closings specifically come from is the key to being more profitable.

The reason to track and measure is obvious: so you will know what to spend MORE time and money on and what to spend less time and money on. I have some agents tell me that they get more closings from referrals, despite their heavy expense in pay per click – but yet they don't actually have a referral marketing system in place. It seems to me like they should spend less on pay per click and more on referral marketing.

Here is a good story: Platinum member Tim J. does a great job of getting must-sell sellers referred over to him, because he did a good job for a handful of people at his Church in getting their upside down home sold. That went viral, word spread. So he continued for a while to get a steady stream of referrals from his church. BUT he never really marketed for them. I suggested he go to his pastor, let him know what he was doing, how some in the congregation had benefitted and offer to do a seminar for anyone in the church that wanted to come, show them how he could help them get out from underneath the pressing home mortgage and get a fresh start. **After a couple seminars, he was group listing 5-10 sellers at each event.** I then suggested he implement a REFER A FRIEND system leveraging the Church Seminar, the "Churched" bringing along the "Unchurched" to the seminar. Good for the church, really good for Tim. **From that he created his Mortgage Maze seminars with expectations of $1 Million in income this year.**

Tim also does a fair amount of marketing for other must-sell sellers, including advertising on the radio and on TV, as well as direct mail. Each one of those ads in those channels say the same thing, **but the call to action is different**. The radio may say go to www . . . .com, the TV www . . . .net, and the direct mail www . . . .info – all landing on the same web page, but he is able to track his response based on different URL's. As a result, he quit doing the radio and television for his mortgage maze seminar and put that money into other more profitable channels. If he had not been tracking it, he would not know where to spend money, and might have concluded that expenses were too high and possibly stopped the seminar altogether.

I have seen many agents go broke with a lot of leads, but never have seen an agent go broke with a lot of appointments. Those that grow a business around appointments – seller appointments and buyer appointments – track what produces leads that lead to appointments. Those that are just after leads, and more or less delegate the leads to outside sales agents, struggle with profitability, or struggle with what to spend money on because they are not sure what is working or where the sales are actually originating from.

If I could wish one thing on a brand new agent just starting out, it would be to learn this lesson of tracking and measuring and put it to work immediately. To know where every lead came from, where appointments came from and when running a sales report, know where each sale originated from. Show me an agent doing that, and I will show you one that is very profitable.

Assumptive Closing Systems that Compel Sellers to List with You!

I was looking at an ad from an agent the other day that was pretty good. It said:

Your Home Sold or I'll Buy It Myself!
000-000-0000 or www . . . .com

Pretty bold statement, but terrible call to action. The agent is assuming sellers will see it, assuming sellers will be so taken back by the offer that they will call or go to the website. So the ad falls short. Way short.

We know that sellers are already skeptical of agents. But obviously this agent is different than others, just based on his statement. But now what? What do you WANT the seller to do? If you want them to call, then tell them to call and what will happen when they do. Same with the website: what will I see or get when I go there.

So the ad better written would be:

Your Home Sold Guaranteed or I'll Buy It at a Price Agreeable to You*
To Find Out How Much You Can Sell Your Home for and How Long it
Will Take Call Todd at 000-000-0000.
If you are not quite ready to talk to Todd directly, request a Free special
report detailing the exclusive Guaranteed Sale Program at www . . . .com

Don't fall short on your marketing, clearly state:

- Here's What I've Got for You
- Here's What it Will do For You
- Here's What I Want You to do Next

We like to say that **a confused mind does nothing.**

Chapter 7
How to Recruit, Hire and Train Your Team

by Craig Proctor

How to Recruit, Hire and Train for Your Highly Profitable Real Estate Sales Team

Background

Even if you are not yet financially at the point of being able to afford an assistant, this is a very important topic for you to be thinking about and planning carefully now. The fact is, every one-man or one-woman show is just a business waiting to happen if you're proactive enough to work on your business to make it happen. If you don't take the time to think about your business; if you spend all your time just doing your business (i.e. working in your business but not on it); you will never get out of the grind you're in. You will forever put in 80-90-100 hours or more per week (until you burn out), and you'll get stuck at a certain level of production that you won't be able to get beyond because you are physically stretched to the limit. Just as bad, the service you give your clients will suffer.

Other People Can Extend Your Capabilities

The right people in the right place at the right time can make things possible. They can extend the capabilities of your business a hundred-fold or more. The key is to develop a system to ensure that you find the right people, place them correctly, train them thoroughly, and motivate them relevantly.

BUT, Your Business Must NOT Be People-Dependent

You may be surprised to learn that the place to start is not with the people themselves. Far from it. While your employees are important individuals on their own, from the standpoint of your business, you must view your Team Members as expendable resources. You see, if your employees weren't replaceable, that would mean that your business depended upon the people you hired -- in other words, that your business was people-dependent.

To understand how dangerous this would be, think about what would happen if you ran a business that was people-dependent and one of your employees became sick and had to take a month or more off. What if an employee became disgruntled and left for another job or, worse, didn't leave, and ended up slowing down and poisoning the process. What would happen to your business in these situations?

The Whole is Greater Than the Sum of the Parts

Now this doesn't mean that the specific individuals you hire are unimportant or that you have a right to treat them poorly or unfairly or with disrespect. It doesn't mean that you should fail to recognize their unique abilities and use these abilities to enhance both their lives and your business. In fact, in my experience, when I recognize and value excellence in my team members, it makes them want to do more for me because they feel acknowledged. They feel acknowledged, and they also feel that they are part of something bigger than themselves. This is the key benefit of a well-functioning "team" -- that is, that the whole is greater than the sum of the parts.

So while the people you hire to join your team are individually important, and while you should welcome and encourage their unique talents and efforts, you MUST NOT become dependent on their special qualities. If you do, you give these team members permission to hold your business hostage. If a team member feels he can threaten your business by withdrawing his or her abilities, you have a problem. You can't leave it up to your team members to invent their jobs and thus your business. A growing business can be crippled by ultimatums such as "give me more money or I'll quit."

Your Business Must Be Position-Driven
NOT People-Dependent

Instead, you must do the inventing, and you must do it before you get help. You must first conceive the position so that your business is position-driven (NOT people-dependent). Then you must have a foolproof plan in place to put a competent person to work in this position, and ensure that you have a system to train, motivate and measure them.

You see, just as you have a duplicatable system for selling a house (post it on MLS, put up a For Sale sign, source leads through your ARPS (Automatic Reverse Prospecting System), etc. etc.), so you need a duplicatable system to build your team. You must begin by recognizing that there are four distinct stages in the process:

- recruiting
- hiring
- training
- managing

Each stage has its own rules and principles, and I will discuss each of these stages separately.

Most agents do NOT have a system for getting help. The first thing that most agents do when they realize that they need help in the form of an assistant is to run out and hire someone -- anyone -- to take some of the pressure off. In actuality, this is the last thing you should do, but like most agents, this is the mistake I made myself.

I Was Quickly Burning Out

When I hired my first assistant, I honestly didn't have a clue what to tell her to do (although I sure kept her busy). I had no organization chart or job description in my head. I just knew I was quickly burning out and needed to share the load with someone. This is very typical of what happens when most agents decide to get help. Even though this wasn't the most effective way to structure my business, it was better than the alternatives which were to either:

1. try to do it all myself, refuse to let any detail slip, and burn myself out in the process, or
2. try to do it all myself, allow some details to slip, and put up with a reality of disgruntled clients and lost prospects

My first assistant found 17 commission cheques shoved in a drawer that I hadn't had time to deposit. Lucky for me, that one simple act on her part more than paid for her salary. Most of you won't be so lucky. The most common problem I hear from agents is that they can't get their assistants to do what they want and, as a result, both their money and time is wasted on someone who is unproductive.

I usually counter to these agents, "Well, what did you WANT your assistant to do?" It sounds like a simple enough question, but it's a thought process very few have gone through, and if you fail to take this important first step, you're almost surely destined for failure with the people you hire.

How Can Your Assistants Do What You Want if You Don't Know What You Want Them to Do?

If you don't have a crystal clear picture of what you want this person to do, how on earth could *they* have an accurate picture. How can they possibly fulfill your expectations if you don't really know what your expectations are?

I Was a Pretty Competent Juggler, but I Was Also Human

In truth, I didn't have any specific expectations of my first assistant. Instead, I just had this vague hope that she would see the balls I fumbled and catch them before they hit the ground. I was a pretty competent juggler, but I was also human, and I really needed someone to catch the overflow because my Automatic Reverse Prospecting System was so effective that I had more business than I alone could handle.

Simply Plugging the Holes is NOT the Same as Planning for the Future

I see now how inefficient these early stages were, but on the plus side, it did initially ease some of the intense pressure I was feeling and allowed me to pause long enough to realize that this was, at best, a way of plugging the holes, but it wasn't a solution that could carry me into a successful future.

The point is, you MUST be very clear about your expectations. You must know specifically what it is that you want your new team member(s) to do. As overworked and overwhelmed as you're feeling (as I was feeling) at the point when you're looking for help, you will compromise the growth of your business from the outset if you haven't taken the time to really understand and map this out.

This may sound like an obvious point, but even the most disciplined among us can fall into the trap of trying to take a shortcut when we're feeling a little stressed and desperate. Actually, it's not just the issue of shortcuts and stress that intervenes and clouds the issue. Sometimes it's an issue of not really knowing what we want someone to do. In my situation, I viewed my job as one big job where everything had to get done. I never thought of it as having several distinct and specific segments to it.

When I began to understand this through my extensive study, it became obvious. But at the time, I just felt stretched and needed someone to help hold me together.

In retrospect, I was very fortunate to be able to overcome my short-sighted disorganization. I was only able to do so by still carrying a superhuman load (a load you may well be carrying yourself right now.) I found that once I'd hired my first assistant, I actually didn't work any less hours.

Instead, I filled the time she freed up to work <u>on</u> my business. I read the *E-Myth* by Michael Gerber cover to cover several times (and I'd recommend you do the same thing if you haven't already done so. It's one of the best business books I've read on business systems.) With long hours, hard work and the insight I'd gained through my experience and study, **I came up with a 9-Step System** (which I'll explain shortly) **which you must follow before you even think about placing a recruitment ad.**

A Team, as defined in my system, is very different from the way traditional real estate companies operate. Rather than a collection of individual agents each working toward separate goals, my Team is a unified group of "specialists" all working toward a common goal.

How Most Agents Operate	My TEAM System
• Undertakes to juggle all these tasks by him/herself	• Your clients get a whole team of professionals working for them (versus a single agent)
• Eventually runs up against the limits of time, energy and money	• As a team, you never run out of time because each Team member is separately responsible for a specific process in the selling of each home
• Few homes sold means limited cash flow to invest back into advertising clients' homes	
• Limited time means less time to spend with clients	• Together, your combined efforts add up to superior marketing and customer service resulting in your homes selling fast and for top dollar

WHAT IS A Rainmaker

In a minute I'm going to refer to the term "Rainmaker". Let me clarify what I mean by this term. In simplest terms, the rainmaker of your business is you -- the one who has the "entrepreneurial spirit" and decided to turn your job into a business. As you can see from the organizational charts in the Forward to this book, the rainmaker (you) is at the center of it all. The only activities you should keep within your realm are those that have the highest return on your time; activities that make you (and your clients) the most amount of money.

There are at least 10 qualities which work together to make a good Rainmaker:

1. **A "Natural" at the Job** - The best rainmakers are "naturals" at the job. They move into situations more easily than most people do. They are comfortable with people. They project self-confidence. They seem to market effortlessly while others struggle to make it happen with far less stellar results.
2. **Intuition** - Rainmakers learn to recognize what really matters most to people. They have a sense of what potential clients REALLY believe is important in choosing an agent.
3. **Good Listener** - Unlike most people, a good rainmaker is a good listener. It is not simply listening that is important, however, but hearing what prospects are saying and making the effort to truly understand their problems or concerns. This is the primary element in building early trust in to the agent/client relationship.
4. **Creative Problem Solvers** - The ability to provide creative solutions elevates a rainmaker to deal maker status. Clients look for programs tailored to their specific needs, not run-of-the-mill solutions that look like, and deliver, the same results as the stuff being churned out by the next five real estate agents down the road. A rainmaker with a positive attitude works to make things happen for a client, not prevent things from happening.
5. **Anticipate Rather Than React** - Rainmakers anticipate, not merely react. They prevent problems instead of figuring out how to deal with them after they occur, and build trust with the client every time they do so.
6. **Extra Effort** - A hallmark trait of a good rainmaker is extra effort, especially as applied to building the client relationship. Service is key, coupled with a concerted effort to "go the extra mile" on the client's behalf.
7. **Put Themselves In Their Clients' Shoes** - Rainmakers put themselves in their clients' shoes. They consider a client's response to everything they do, and make sure the client fully understands what is being planned and executed on his/her behalf.
8. **Never Bluffs** - A good rainmaker never claims to know what he doesn't know . . . but s/he always finds out what s/he doesn't know and gives that answer to the client as quickly as s/he can.

9. **Sees and Is Seen** - "See and Be Seen". This should be the Rainmaker's Watchword. Maintaining a high community profile by joining local business groups and charitable boards reflects well on the rainmaker.
10. **Entrepreneurial** - Rainmakers need to be entrepreneurial, willing to take risks. They know playing it safe doesn't develop new business, and they work hard to create opportunities. If they don't leap at these opportunities, they know someone else will.

If you are a rainmaker like this, count your lucky stars. Remember that, ultimately, the one widely shared trait of good rainmakers everywhere is energy and lots of it. It has to be focused and goal oriented, but without that high level of energy, your rainmaker is just another soggy salesperson.

The 9 Step Strategic Process

You have to take a giant step back and design your ideal team (You may envision your team as just you and one unlicensed assistant, you and one buyer's agent, or you at the helm of a large team.) and how you will go about building it (The Strategy). In the following sections, I'll show you how to make it all happen (The Execution) which includes not only recruiting and hiring them, but also training and managing them.

I'll lead you through the thought-process of how to go about hiring staff before you actually begin to recruit.

As discussed above, after much study and thought, I developed a 9 step system which outlines the steps and thinking you must go through to prepare you for success in growing your business with team support.

The Strategy

Building Your Team - The 9 Step System

1. **Determine your strengths** - take the D-I-S-C personality test to identify what your strengths and weaknesses are.
2. **Define your Rainmaker role** - given your understanding of what parts of your business you can change the outcome of, create a position contract for your job as Rainmaker
3. **Determine your worth per hour** - How much money do you make in a year? How many hours do you work in a year? Divide one by the other to determine your worth per hour.

4. **Isolate the activities you shouldn't be doing** - Isolate all the activities that you could pay someone less than your worth per hour to do. Categorize these activities into definable jobs or positions.

5. **Create a blank organizational chart** - This is your blueprint for your future Team. You are probably doing most of these jobs yourself. As your business grows, you will hire people to fill the positions and replace your name with theirs.

6. **Design your "game worth playing"** - determine in an overall sense what game you will ask new Team members to play. The idea of this game will help you outline the next step

7. **Develop written position contracts** - for each box on your organizational chart, write a detailed and specific description of what this job would entail. Remember to build cross-training into these positions so you'll never get caught holding the bag if one of your team members is absent or quits. This way your business becomes position-driven rather than people-dependent.

8. **Decide which order you will fill the positions in and when** - considering the needs of your business and your financial situation, decide which team members you need first, second, third and so on. Remember, this is a step-by-step process. Few agents will be able to build an entire team overnight.

9. **Execute your plan** - now it's time to make it happen. Put your plan into effect to get great people on board who are ready, willing and able to make great things happen for your business. The execution of your plan is called the T-E-A-M system.

Your Blank Organizational Chart

The blank boxes you identify in the strategic stage are a collection of like tasks and duties that you will eventually assign to a new team member who will "specialize" in these functions.

Let me give you an example of the kinds of positions I identified for my business once I went through the process just outlined. Many of the things I did in a day related to assembling, coordinating and disseminating information about my listings. I found that I needed one person who could co-ordinate all listing information (i.e. gather the details and write up the descriptions, place the ads in proper rotation and generally keep track of what was happening on each listing), kind of like an office quarterback.

To do these duties, this person would NOT have to be licensed. I hired Cindy to take care of these functions several years ago. Cindy didn't have to find or present to prospects. She didn't have to bang on doors or bang in signs or give customer feedback. Instead, she became highly focused on this narrow and related range of activities and thus did a great job of them. They always got done perfectly and in the correct way.

Importantly, because all the systematic details of Cindy's job as Listing Co-ordinator were clearly documented and laid out (in the Position Contract for this position), if Cindy were to leave short or long-term, I could easily recruit, hire, train and manage someone else in this position.

Another position which fell out of my analysis was that of Customer Service Manager. I found I needed a licensed person to help with customer service after clients had signed a contract with me. I eventually hired Brenda to do this job. Brenda followed up with each of my clients on a weekly basis to give them feedback on showings etc. She was great at nurturing these relationships and ensuring my clients felt acknowledged and informed. While I was free to do what I did best, which is to convert prospects to clients, I knew there was a reliable system in place which would ensure my clients were happy.

Like Cindy, Brenda was free to focus her time and attention around a few, related activities. They became specialists in these positions, and because the position descriptions were reasonably narrow, they could be systemized into repetitive steps or responsibilities which could easily be taken over by someone else should the need arise.

I Hired "Average" People

Let me make an important point here. My Team consisted of a few extraordinary people, but mostly average people. You have to be able to build your business with these average people by giving them a narrow range of tasks which are within their capabilities.

Take the example of McDonalds, which is where Gerber professes to have got his inspiration. Ray Croc, the founder of McDonalds was, to be sure, an extraordinary entrepreneur. When McDonalds became a franchise, the company suddenly required thousands of employees to run all the restaurants which sprang up.

When you think in terms of "thousands" of employees, you realize that it's unlikely that you'll find "thousands" of extraordinary people. Instead, you'll have to break down the tasks to their lowest common denominator, and ensure that average people can excel at them. If you expect too much of people, expect to be disappointed.

When McDonalds hires a hamburger flipper, they don't expect the hamburger flipper to be super-intelligent or super entrepreneurial. They don't require the hamburger flipper to have a great personality or know how to manage the restaurant. They just want the hamburger flipper to do a really great job of flipping hamburgers. After all, it's unlikely that a person who could be content flipping hamburgers would have the skills to do these other jobs anyway.

But Mr. Croc doesn't care about this. He knows that if one hamburger flipper leaves, his business won't be paralyzed -- he'll just go out and hire some other unskilled worker and teach them how to flip hamburgers the McDonalds way.

I Was Expecting Too Much of Outside Sales Agents

Your business has to operate on the same principles. Let me give you an example. At one time, as my ARPS became more and more finely tuned, I found that my needs with respect to my team members also changed. As more and more leads poured into my office, I initially theorized that the need for an Inside Sales Agent was becoming obsolete. I no longer needed team members to source prospects since this was happening automatically. My initial vision was that these leads would be handed directly to my Outside Sales Agents for follow up in the same way that I followed up with these leads. The process excited me because the time I spent on the phone each day with prospects was much more fruitful (because the prospects were much better qualified), and my transactions increased dramatically, and I assumed my Outside Sales Agents would have the same experience.

Instead, what also increased dramatically (I discovered over time) was the bleeding (i.e. many leads generated by my ARPS (Automatic Reverse Prospecting System) were being lost because of inadequate follow-up by my Outside Sales Agents.) The fact is, while I had some OSAs who would follow up on some of the leads some of the time, as a general rule they weren't very good at follow up.

At first this made me frustrated (frustration is often the mother of invention.) Why couldn't they just follow up on these leads I asked myself (and them.) They don't have to do any cold-calling. All they have to do is nurture and keep in touch with warm leads -- people who had expressed the intent to buy or sell in the near future.

But here's where I had to face a hard reality and let my business evolve to reflect this reality. You see, even though you and I may have the discipline to do all parts of the job, the kind of person who comes to work for you probably doesn't have your vision and drive. (If they did, they'd be trying to build a business on their own.) As I hope I've made clear, it would also be dangerous to depend on the personality of someone who could put all the parts together.

While I had a couple of really dynamite OSAs who willingly went the extra mile, for the most part, my Outside Sales Agents simply wanted to work with "now" business, NOT follow-up the future business.

I Finally Realized That These Were Two Different Jobs Requiring Two Different Kinds of People

Were these people lazy? At first I felt they were, but as I allowed my paradigm to shift, I came to realize that the "follow-up" and the "face-to-face nurturing" are really two different personality strengths that probably don't reside together in many individuals.

The fact is, the most successful realtors are those who have some high combination of D (Dominance) and I (influence). They're charismatic, aggressive, self-starting and persuasive. In neither of these personality profiles is there a high tolerance for detail work or repetition. No wonder my licensed OSAs did a crummy job of follow-up.

My Inside Sales Agents, on the other hand, have some D and I (i.e. they like working with people and aren't pushovers,) but they also have a healthy share of C (Compliance) which means they are attentive to detail and good with follow-up.

I realized I was expecting too much of my OSAs, and my business suffered because of it. So I restructured the Inside Sales Agents' and Outside Sales Agents' positions to improve the process.

This is how it works now in the businesses of the agents I coach. My Inside Sales Agents (i.e. what I used to call Telemarketers -- agents who want a more predictable, orderly existence and have a higher tolerance for details and follow-up work) are responsible for nurturing the warm leads which emerge from my ARPS. They work a fixed 40 hour week with a decent guaranteed salary (they love this security and stability) plus commission on any warm leads which they can nurture into hot leads that buy or sell a home.

Once a prospect is ready-to-act, they're handed over to one of the OSAs (or to the Rainmaker if it's a seller prospect) who takes over the friendly, face-to-face meetings and presentations. This agent would ensure that this client feeds into all parts of our system and emerges a happy client at the other end.

These are four of the positions you'll find on the organizational chart in this book's Forward. While my Outside Sales Agents and Inside Sales Agents help to drive business by aiding in the prospect conversion stage, the other team members are just as vital as they flawlessly take care of all the minute but essential details which are necessary for the day-to-day functioning of the business.

So where do you get these people, and how do you ensure they do what they're supposed to do? That's the subject of the next four sections which outline the execution of the strategy you've just explored and mapped out.

The Execution

The Team System

Tell The World You're Looking for Team Members
(The Recruiting System)

Entertain Interested Candidates and Choose the Best
(The Hiring System)

Allow Them to Learn Before Doing
(The Training System)

Manage Your Team
(The Managing System)

The Recruiting System

Tell The World You're Looking For Team Members

Now you have a chart with empty boxes. And you have a playbook (your position contracts) which defines in detailed terms what each of these boxes is responsible for. Your next step is to determine which is the most critical box to fill first - i.e. where is your greatest need.

The first thing you'll need to do is find candidates who could potentially fill the position(s) you are recruiting for. You'll find these candidates in exactly the same way you should be finding buyer and seller prospects, with your ARPS (Automatic Reverse Prospecting System) - i.e. you'll place an ad that will compel candidates to contact you, and then to jump through the hoop of sending you their resume. By asking candidates to send a resume, you'll be able to assess much more quickly which ones you want to take forward to the next step.

A successful ad will draw a high number of queries. The more people you have to choose from, the better the chance that you'll find someone good.

In the next section - The Hiring System - I'll tell you how to sift through all the people who reply to find the candidate(s) who will do the best job for you.

The Hiring System

Entertain Interested Candidates and Choose the Best

The purpose of this system is to put all the candidates into the "funnel" and then sift out the best - i.e. the one(s) you want to hire. As I'm sure you realize, this exactly parallels the process I use to sift out the best home buyer/homeseller prospects via my website and hotline.

Part of the interviewing process should include the DISC personality test which is like a DNA test of someone's personality, and will help you chose people whose personality naturally fits the position(s) you have created.

Many agents make the mistake of hiring someone just like themselves. Don't do this. You should hire assistants to complement your rainmaker skills - don't hire someone just like you. The role of your assistants is to perform the tasks that free you, as Rainmaker, to focus on activities where you can change the outcome.

My personal finding is that most successful agents are High D and I personalities. Here are some examples of the personalities which best fit some of the team members you will need to hire:

Outside Sales Agents .... High I with D

Inside Sales Agents .... High C with D and I

Call Coordinator .... High S or C with I

Customer Service Manager .... High S with D and I

Database Management .... High C

Bookkeeper .... High C

Office Manger .... High I with D, S and C

My 10 Step Hiring System

I have a ten step system that I use to hire new team members. My goal is to attract a lot of interest with my ad, but I don't want to waste a lot of my time with those who probably would never work out. I get my office administrator to manage the parts of the interviewing process that I don't need to be involved in, and then have a system in place whereby the candidates will sift themselves in or out of the next steps. I will interview only those that I consider highly qualified candidates.

These 10 steps help you follow the process systematically, efficiently and objectively to give you the best opportunity of finding the best candidate for the job.

1. **Review the resumes** (if a candidate does not have a prepared resume, I won't even consider them)
2. **Select those candidates** who will be invited in for an interview
3. Have my assistant phone respondents and **set up a time and date when all candidates will come in together for stage one** of the interviewing process
4. Put all respondents in the boardroom, and have my assistant **administer the personality tests** to them
5. Have my assistant **score these tests**
6. I then **present my vision** to this group of respondents. I tell them about my company and about the position they are applying for. I explain what is expected of them, and what's in it for them. I'm very blunt and candid at this stage. I tell them exactly what I will

      do for them and what I expect them to do for me. In this way, only those who are truly interested in the position will move on. There will be no surprises down the road.

7. Have the candidates **fill out a form** which indicates whether, on the basis of what they have heard, they want to be considered for the next stage of the interviewing process.

8. I **review the personality tests** of the candidates who have expressed an interest in going on to the next stage, and choose the ones I am most interested in.

9. These candidates are called in for **individual interviews** with me.

10. I make an **offer of employment** to one or more of the candidates (if they match what I'm looking for).

The Training System

Allow Them to Learn Before Doing

The sad fact of the matter is, once most agents hire someone to help them, they completely let go and somehow expect the new assistant to know exactly what to do and to have the same dedication and work ethic that they have. This rarely happens.

The fatal mistake that most real estate agents make is to leave things to chance once they've made a decision to hire an assistant. The relief is so great to have another body to share the work load with, that the tendency is to split the pressure and run in opposite directions. This is a recipe for disaster, and one which many of you have surely encountered. Before too long, the employee who was supposed to be your savior is just another headache you have to deal with because they're not performing the way you wanted them to perform.

But ask yourself -- how did you want them to perform? Did you lay it our clearly? Did you show them, tell them, work with them to make sure they understood what was expected of them and train them in areas specific to the skills necessary for superior execution of the position they are filling? Probably not.

Training is a sorely neglected task in most organizations and, as a result, instead of decreasing, your workload increases. The problem is, you tell yourself, "I'm so busy doing my own job, I don't have time to babysit my new assistant -- I want them to help me!"

However, unless you take some upfront time with a new employee, you'll more than likely be hanging an albatross around your neck that will slow you down even more. It's the same old working *on* your business vs. *in* it preaching I've been doing. And it's important for the very same reasons.

But here's the good news. While the training portion may be time consuming first time round, it's time invested in your future. By creating a system to train a new employee, you create a duplicatable program that will be easy when you hire the second, third and subsequent person in that position.

Use the position contract for your new employee's job to create a map for how you will train them step-by-step. Sit with your new people and talk through exactly what you expect of them. Set clear goals with clear time lines. If the assistant is an agent, have them shadow you in your listing presentations, negotiations, offers etc. Make sure you give them adequate work space to learn in (even if it's only temporary).

Introduce them to fellow team members. Collect and organize some training material for them to get through which will give them needed knowledge for the job they have taken on. Compile both internal documents generated by your office and my system manuals to give them both a specific sense of your office, and a big picture view for where they fit in. A few hours spent now will save you days and weeks and thousands of dollars later. The only way you will ever realize the exponential power of leverage with respect to your assistants is if you properly train them from their first moment on the job. Before you know it, this part of your job will be much less time consuming and you'll be free to attack all the neglected areas of your business that you hired this person to free you up for.

Never Assume Anything

A good rule of thumb is to never assume anything. If the new team member is a quick study, you can move through the steps of the training process more quickly, but don't leave any steps out. What's obvious to you because you're living and breathing your business may not be obvious to the person you hire.

It's a good idea to establish a probation or trial period upfront (usually 3-6 months depending on the position.) Let the Team member know that you'll meet formally on a certain date to mutually review progress to determine if you are meeting each other's expectations.

If you omit the critical step of training new team members, you will almost certainly end up in a situation where they will quit (or you will fire them.) It's just a matter of time. Without training, you'll likely find yourself back at the drawing board, having to recruit all over again.

The Managing System

Manage Your Team

Many agents manage their employees using the principle of Seagull Management:

- **SWOOP** into the office
- **SQUAWK** a bunch of commands at your assistants
- **FLY** out of the office before they can ask questions
- **SWOOP** back into the office
- **CRAP** all other them when they tell you that your commands could not be completed

SEAGULL MANAGEMENT

This is because they have no clear system to ensure that their assistants are doing the right things and doing them well. As a result, they worry constantly as things don't get done, and they end up doing everyone's job and managing by crisis.

It doesn't have to be that way. Managing your employees doesn't mean doing their jobs. You have hired them to free you to do other things. While managing them will have to be one of the things you do (unless you delegate this to someone else), the role of manager doesn't have to be time-consuming. If you've trained them properly, and if you've set up clear and measurable parameters that you can monitor them by, then you can track their performance objectively, fairly and easily (in exactly the same way you do with your advertising).

Part of the issue I'm talking about here is effective communication. Assuming that you've followed the steps and strategies outlined to recruit, hire and train, every single one of your team members should have a crystal clear understanding of what you expect of them, both on a day-to-day basis, and longer term. In order that these expectations are met, you need to:

- Ensure that two-way communication occurs regularly and formally (I held a mandatory Monday morning meeting with all staff to review objectives, performance, and updates.)
- Incorporate an objective system of measurement in the form of performance reports to monitor long term achievements of your Team members, and
- Incorporate a management strategy that ensures that day-to-day duties are being carried out without you having to worry about them.

Through my study of other industries, I discovered a unique, but highly effective, management strategy which I used in my own business called Management by Exception. This important concept will allow you to get on with the business of working on your business with the peace of mind that things are getting done without your constant interference.

Management by Exception

Management by Exception is one of those common sense concepts that I'm sure 99% don't practice. It is a management system which assumes that work is done according to orchestrated systems and standards. Any exception to the sanctioned orchestration requires notification of the manager in the form of an exception report. The exception report provides the nature of the exception, the logic and, if appropriate, an alternative strategy, due date, or request for assistance.

As you can see, this concept assumes a perfectly visioned and detailed system. There's no guesswork required on the part of your people -- they have been told exactly what to do and how to do it. They will, therefore, be able to operate the system perfectly -- without you. There will be no need for them to constantly ask you questions about this or that. There will be no need for you to watch over their shoulders. You'll be able to focus on working on the business knowing that everything is running smoothly and exactly as it should -- and if it isn't, you'll hear about it.

Furthermore, you'll hear about the exception not in the form of a problem you will have to drop your work to solve, but rather in the form of a solution -- a notification of the deviation and how it was solved.

Managing With Questions

You should make it your business to learn from your team members as well as they will come to know their functions better than you ever will. Their feedback and opinions will be input to your ultimate role which is to constantly improve the overall system.

Therefore, effectively managing your team members should involve asking questions . . . lots of questions. Here are 10 great questions you should be asking team members as you talk with them throughout the course of a normal day.

As an entrepreneur, most of these questions will be ones you find yourself unconsciously asking yourself all the time. Your team members, however, probably won't think these questions through unless you ask them.

1. What made you mad today?
2. What took too long?
3. What caused complaints today?
4. What was misunderstood today?
5. What cost too much?
6. What was wasted?
7. What was too complicated?
8. What was just plain silly?
9. What job involved too many people?
10. What job involved too many actions?

Not only will this send the important message to your team that their opinions matter, you'll also be surprised at how enlightening some of their opinions are. The most important concept in effective management is to help your team members take responsibility for a common definition of success. I read an interesting article recently which stated this same concept in a different way and stressed the critical importance of delegation.

Management by Delegation

Do these scenarios sound familiar? You're walking to your office and an employee stops you to give you a rundown of what's happening: "I phoned the paper to place the ad you wanted and the rep won't get back to me. So I'm going to try again tomorrow morning and spend the balance of the day following up the leads I was trying to get to last week. I should have reached most of them by next Tuesday, and, by the way, the copy machine is broken. Should I call a repairman?"

As you get to your office, another Team Member stops you to give a rundown of his or her situation. This lasts another three minutes.

Frustrating? You bet. And you wonder, why can't these people take more responsibility and not drop every detail of every project in your lap?

Well, maybe it's not them, but you. Maybe you're not delegating effectively. Here are some key points to remember:

1. **Stress results, not details**. Make it clear to your team members that you're more concerned about the final outcome of all projects, rather than the day-to-day details that accompany them.

2. **Don't be sucked into giving solutions to team members' problems**. When team members come to you with problems, they're probably looking for you to solve them. Don't. Teach them how to solve problems themselves. This, too, can be frustrating because it takes time. But in the long run, you'll save yourself time and money.

3. **Turn the question around**. If a team member comes to you with a problem, ask him or her for possible solutions. If a team member comes to you with a question, ask for possible answers.

4. **Establish measurable and concrete objectives**. With all team members, make your objectives clear and specific. Once this is done, they will feel more comfortable acting on their own. Think of this plan as a road map -- and your team members will too.

5. **Develop reporting systems.** Get your feedback from reporting systems: monthly reports, statistical data, or samplings (I recommend weekly meetings with team members.)

6. **Give strict and realistic deadlines**. If you don't give clear deadlines, team members won't feel accountable for the completion of their tasks.

7. **Keep a delegation log.** When you delegate an assignment, jot it down. You'll be able to monitor the progress, and discipline team members when necessary.

8. **Recognize the talents and personalities of your team members**. Being a good delegator is like being a good coach of a baseball team. You have to know what projects each team member can handle, and what projects they can't.

Summing up, there are three main parts to the whole of managing my team which I call my CAR formula:

Communication – in the form of weekly team meetings to measure, Inform and update

Accountability – through effective delegation and management by exception, make team members responsible for their day-to-day functions

Reporting – weekly, monthly and yearly reports objectively measure whether a team member is making it happen

When you manage your car effectively, it will go and go and go (and so will your team and, as a result, so will your business.)

Part 2

Chapter 8
Proof of Results

by Todd Walters

Since the mid 90's, Craig Proctor Real Estate Coaching has helped thousands of agent's quantum leap their business . . . many so much so that they have built and are building highly profitable real estate sales team businesses. In the previous chapters you have heard from Craig and me about establishing and leveraging your very own team to not only sell more homes, but give superior service and results to clients. But . . . there is no need to simply take our word for it.

On the following pages you will read about others who have built amazingly successful real estate sales team businesses. These contributing authors to this book are members of our coaching programs at Craig Proctor Real Estate Coaching. They have effectively taken what Craig and I give and teach and put it to work in their own businesses, **allowing them to establish highly profitable real estate businesses that do not depend on their constant involvement**. These agents only do the things they are good at, while delegating (not abdicating) everything else to their award winning team of professionals.

I have often heard Craig say, "Success Leaves Clues". For that reason you would be wise to study each of these Team Leaders' words and how they do things. More importantly than "how" is what they think about each day, because what you think about and how you think about things directly impacts your level of success. I kid around at conferences and on coaching consults with agents telling them that I would sit around my office and think about how NOT to do things, but still get everything done, while giving superior service and results to clients. I am not really kidding though. To an extent it is true, and this way of thinking translates into "leverage", allowing way more to get done and get done way better than ONE agent doing all the work.

So as you read what some of our most successful members from around North America have to say about their team and how they do things, remember that they approach this business from a different paradigm than the majority of real estate agents do.

Enjoy their words! I know I do and am regularly inspired by them.

Chapter 9
Success Leaves Clues

by Rudy Kusuma & Todd Walters

One of the points Craig and I make throughout our time coaching agents is to study success. But let me be clearer on this point here.

Success comes in many different forms and manifests in many different types of people, personalities, races, religious preferences, man, woman. But, what is real success?

There have been a lot of books written on this subject and I mean a lot over a long period of time. For me, success is demonstrated by someone who is at the pinnacle of whatever I most want to do or accomplish. They do 'IT' seemingly better than the vast majority of others, and . . . this is important, they carry it well.

It's one thing to be really, really good at something, but another to mismanage how it's displayed. No one really wants to learn from a bad or corrupt or self-indulged person.

Obviously, because you're reading this book, you're someone who is motivated by success. You believe there is more that can be obtained. You get a charge out of, and are inspired by, those who overcome hardships and go on to become uber successful.

I know many real estate agents that fit this category. One that jumps to the front of my mind is Rudy Kusuma. Rudy is one of the top RE/MAX Agents in California. His team is spectacular, and they do fantastic work for buyers and sellers in the L.A. area. This is a man to study.

*His story is both inspiring and FULL of clues to being more successful, and to establishing a highly profitable real estate sales team. Read his story with a highlighter or note pad. – **Todd Walters***

✦ ✦ ✦

A Success Story

by Rudy Lira Kusuma

Introduction:

I was born and raised in Indonesia, and at the age of 12, my parents sent me to Singapore for my middle and high school. After I graduated, they sent me to the United States for my college education. I started off at Santa Monica College in Southern California, before transferring to the University of Wisconsin in Madison for my Bachelor of Science degree in Mathematics. My parents' dream had been for their son to work in a Big Corporation, receiving a huge pay check with all the benefits. They considered that a "safe harbor". I completed my undergraduate university education in less than 3.5 years, and was accepted at the School of Mathematics Graduate program at the California State University in Los Angeles, on scholarship. After reading the book *Rich Dad Poor Dad* by Robert Kiyosaki, I understood the drawbacks of working for someone else instead of building your own business. Needless to say, I withdrew my enrollment form and started taking all the sales courses and seminars that I could get my hands on. I was a seminar junkie.

I got involved in a series of networking companies just to get some sales skills. I started my basic training with hours of cold calling and door knocking, where I was chased by dogs more than a couple of times. Tell you the truth, I hated it. I couldn't stand rejection, and I almost gave up a few times. But when you persevere, you learn from each failure.

Beginning of my Real Estate Career:

In February 2007, I was trying to sell legal insurance to a church member who owned "ERA" real estate company. He didn't buy my product, but instead told me I could be a really good real estate agent. So I gave it a try. I took the test, passed it and joined his real estate brokerage. I started my real estate career when the market had just tanked and no tools were provided to help me get started. So I began by door knocking and passing out flyers, because I didn't know what else to do.

Since I didn't have any clients, and I had a lot of time, I started hosting Robert Kiyosaki's cashflow club, and expanded that to Investor's club. To this day, our Team NuVision Investor's Club has over 1,357 members. We got assignment deals from this club alone that has netted us over $200,000 in income.

My very first shot at a real estate transaction was my friend's short sale deal. I knew nothing about signing a listing agreement, let alone a short sale transaction. The broker that I was with provided very little direction, so I had to look somewhere else for knowledge. Wanting to understand this process, I started taking short sale courses. While I wanted to continue to work on increasing my knowledge in the field of real estate, I was extremely disappointed that in all of 2007 I didn't sell any homes.

I moved to a different Coldwell Banker brokerage in mid 2008 and again there was no training. The only "training" provided centered on cold calling and door knocking and I hated both. So while I continued to work hard, I also began searching for a better and more systematic training that would allow me to build my business.

In 2008, I sold 8 homes, averaging about $60,000 in commission while working 60 hours per week. The next year, I managed to increase my income to $110,000, but was now putting in 80+ hours per week.

In 2010, I don't even know how many hours I was putting in per week, more than the previous year, and I made $250,000. I had a newborn baby at home who I hardly ever saw and this pushed me to realize that I had to do something to reduce the hours I was putting in at work. I hired my first assistant, thinking 2011 would be better.

2011 did change but not in the way I had hoped. I had 1 assistant and 2 outside sales people and I made $350,000 in commissions. My OSA handled buyers, but because I didn't provide training or tools, we were shooting blindly. I was working extremely hard and doing the best I could but was having to constantly replace my OSA's because I didn't know how to create value to retain good people . . . a classic problem. I was desperate for a coaching program that could help me turn my estate career from a job, into a true business.

Beginning of Building a True Real Estate Business (vs. a Career)

In the spring on 2012, I found a flyer at my office advertising a "Craig Proctor" seminar. I went to the half-day seminar and signed up for the 3-day seminar in Anaheim. The seminar was great and I excitedly returned to my marketplace with all these new tools. I thought I would be making my first million in that same year, but I quit after 6 months. Not because the program didn't work, but because it was too overwhelming for me. I didn't have enough manpower to implement all the programs and handle all the business.

In March 2012, my second son was born. My wife quit her job, saying she wanted to go back to Indonesia to live and would spend her time working in her family's business. She was burnt out from working 9-5, making $50K per year and having a husband who was never home.

After discussing our situation we agreed that we would send our 9-month old son to live with our family in Indonesia while she would help me in our business. She gave me 1 year to prove that we could really turn our business around.

I took her to a Craig Proctor conference in LA that year. The whole thing made sense to her, so we agreed that we would get really serious and implement the coaching program into our business. It wasn't without struggle; it's a constant learning experience, but I can tell you, it didn't take us 1 year to see our 1st million. In March of 2013, we joined the Craig Proctor Platinum Program. Once we joined the Platinum Program, our coach, Todd, helped us to take our business to a brand new level. One program that works exceptionally well for us in our marketplace is the Guaranteed Sale Program.

By the end of 2013, we had 5 Outside Sales Agents, sold 115 homes, with $1 million in GCI, and we brought home our second son from Indonesia in November, 2013.

Now that our business is running so well, we are enjoying the recognition that comes with our hard-earned success. We had the honor of receiving the Craig Proctor $1Million income earner award in 2013. In February, 2014, at the Re/Max International convention, I was awarded the Hall of Fame award which recognizes those who earn more than $1 million GCI.

But it got better even than that. Our team was recognized at the RE/MAX Convention in March 2015 as: #1 in San Gabriel Valley, Top 5 in California, Top 50 in the United States, and Top 100 in the world. In addition to that, our team was also recognized as the "2014 Miracle Office" for being the top contributor to the Children's Hospital in Los Angeles.

Game Changers in Our Business

1. **Using Statistics in our JS Postcard – leveraging the Guaranteed Sale program** - The very first conference call I had with Todd, I remember he said, "You sent me all these marketing pieces, but I don't see your USP, and I don't see a reason why I should do business with you". I found that profound. He asked us, "Why should I do business with you, over anybody else, including selling the house myself?" I was dumbfounded. That was the beginning of my decision to learn more about what the Guaranteed Sale Program is about, and truly being able to leverage it better in our marketplace. I couldn't even guess at how many times my phone has rung and a prospect has asked me, "How much will you buy my house for?" My answer is always the same, "I don't know, when can I come over and take a look at your house?" Thanks to the great coaches we have, I am able to book listing appointments just from this simple conversation.

2. **Hiring an ISA** - Hiring an ISA to follow up with the leads that we generate was a real money-maker and time saver for us. Very early on during our participation in the Craig Proctor coaching program we were taught how to generate leads. So our problem wasn't in generating leads, it was in how to convert those leads to appointments and appointments to closings. Hiring an Inside Sales Agent was like finding a missing piece of the puzzle. Now, the results are predictable and we are able to measure our marketing dollars. Like Craig and Todd say, "If you can't measure it, you shouldn't do it".

I often hear people say, making your first $1 million is the hardest, but after that, it's like a snowball, it gets easier once you hit your first million, and I certainly agree. I finally understand what it means to "work less and make more money", as quoted by my two great coaches.

 **Rudy L. Kusuma** is the Founder and CEO of RE/MAX TITANIUM and the Managing Director of TEAM NUVISION, The #1 Real Estate Sales Team in San Gabriel Valley. He was recently selected as a Dave Ramsey Endorsed Local Provider and enjoys consulting with San Gabriel Valley sellers and buyers with the heart of a teacher, not a salesperson. Rudy has been hosting weekly real estate educational workshops for home buyers, sellers, and investors since 2007.

Rudy is the recipient of the 2013, 2014, and 2015 Five Star Real Estate Agent Award. This level of excellence is achieved by less than 7% of the real estate agents in California. Rudy has been recognized as the #1 Top Producer since 2007. Rudy and his team have sold over $100 Million in transactions. RE/MAX International recently named him #1 in San Gabriel Valley, Top 5 in California, Top 50 in the United States, and Top 100 in the world (out of 97,000 agents.)

Rudy has the passion, knowledge, and experience to help homeowners avoid foreclosure. He specializes in complex transactions representing owners in disposition of their assets. In today's real estate market, he has successfully negotiated more than $30 million of distressed sales with lenders nationwide, including Bank of America, Wachovia, Wells Fargo, Citi Mortgage, CHASE, Bank of The West, East West Bank, HSBC, and many more.

Rudy lives in Temple City with his wife and two sons. He's a homeowner, investor, and holds California Real Estate Broker License 01820322.

You can reach Rudy online at www.TeamNuVision.net or by telephone at 626-780-2221

Chapter 10
From Marine to Millionaire Agent

by Jim Bottrell

How a Former Marine Turned Real Estate Agent Uses Leadership – Vision, Organization, and Systems to Establish a Millionaire Real Estate Sales Team.

"How did you go from being a Marine to owning a real estate company? They are so different!" people always ask once they find out that I was a Major in the United States Marine Corps before starting a real estate company.

I always reply exactly the same by saying, "Well, as weird as it sounds, the two roles are almost entirely the same. In the Marine Corps, my job was to manage people, processes, and provide solid leadership. As the owner of a real estate company, my job is to manage people, processes, and provide solid leadership. The key difference between the two is that it's pretty unlikely that somebody will shoot at us when we sell houses," . . . which always receives a laugh.

"How did you know how to build your company so fast?" is the next question about 90% of the time.

I explain to them that I sought out some very smart people that taught me how to implement repeatable and predictable systems, even in the chaotically unpredictable environment of real estate. That once we implemented those systems, we more than doubled our revenue, then we more than doubled it again the next year.

What I don't mention in those conversations for obvious reasons is that we went from a $200,000 GCI (Gross Commission Income) to $1,000,000 CGI in just over 24 months. The good news for you is that I'm about to tell you how we did it . . .

One thing that I need to address at this time is that any United States Marine that read my answer above just cringed in horror because I used the word "Manage" to describe what I did in the two jobs. In the Marine Corps, we call managing "The M Word" as it is almost forbidden and demands as much disrespect as any word can. The reason being that there is a big difference between "Managing" and "Leading". Those differences were pounded into our heads early on in Boot Camp and literally as we got off the bus at Officer Candidates School.

So why am I talking about Leadership in a book about real estate? Let me explain:

It's actually pretty simple. No matter where you work, what you do, or how you do it; people will gravitate to you if you do what you do confidently, with purpose, are consistent, and you listen. The interesting part is that WHAT the leader is doing is actually less important than HOW he is doing it. Everything must be done with confidence, purpose, and consistency. "A poor plan executed violently is superior to a great plan executed poorly," is what I can still hear my Marine Corps Drill Instructors screaming over and over again. So, maybe for this context, we replace the word "violently" with "correctly".

Confidence in the way you speak, your actions, even in the way you walk from point A to point B. Do each of those with purpose and confidence and you will be surprised how easily things happen for you. In its most simplified form, those are the most critical elements of Leadership.

A Leader is a person that people look up to. People want to emulate or ascend to the same level. Not because a Leader is flawless by any means, but because the Leader is decisive in actions yet caring and compassionate to others and listens to their needs. A leader does not just look at what he can make people do, a Leader uses systems in a very consistent way to get things done because people WANT to do those tasks vs. being made to do those tasks.

Managing, on the other hand, derives its "power" more from a job title than anything else. People do things for the manager because they have to – because the manager is the boss. It says so on his/her office door, on their business cards, etc. The point is that people do things for the manager because they *have* to, while they do things for a Leader because they *want* to. Just one of the reasons why the word "Managing" is so vehemently despised in the Marine Corps.

So back to real estate . . .

For me, I quickly learned that I had advantages in real estate because of my years being a "Leader of Marines". I, just like the majority of agents, started my career in real estate largely as a Buyer's agent. Long weekends showing homes, preparing for those showings, doing open houses etc., etc., etc. All of the stuff that newer agents do. However, it didn't take me long to realize that I was able to sell houses to my Buyers quicker than my peers could.

"How did you put them in a house so quickly?" my peers often asked. Sometimes not so nicely . . .

It was actually fairly simple: I was organized, on time to everything ("if you are not 5 minutes early, you are late!"), did what I said I was going to do (every single time) and acted confidently and decisively. If you do those simple things, people will trust you. If they trust you, they feel more confident making decisions around you. I never had to "sell" my clients on anything. They correctly trusted in me that I would not allow them to go down the wrong path. Therefore, they found it easy to make decisions around me. That meant they bought houses quicker. You can do the same thing.

The other advantage that I had, which truly changed my business, was that I was not too proud to put down my own rather large ego and LISTEN. In this case, I'm talking about listening to somebody point out the flaws of my business. Sometimes hard to hear that you are doing it wrong, or more to my personal situation, that I was not seeing what was right in front of me . . . Staring me in the face.

The good news is that I listened to the coaches that I hired to help me organize and build my business. Not just any coaches though – my coaches had built multi-million dollar real estate businesses of their own. I believe it's important who you learn from – for me, they MUST be people that have succeeded in exactly what I was trying to succeed at. In my case, I hired Craig Proctor and Todd Walters. These two spent years as the number one and number two RE/MAX® agents in the world. They built their businesses from the ground up, making mistakes along the way, correcting them, building systems, and kicking-ass. I found a wealth of knowledge in these two. From that point forward, my business, and my life, took a substantially different path than it ever would have without them.

Vision:

Once I saw the Vision that Craig and Todd were talking about, it made me look at the entire real estate industry differently. More of a true Business vs. a highly leveraged job. When I was making $200,000 per year I thought I was Top-Dog! On top of the world! I thought I had reached my "Blue Skies" and there wasn't much more I could do.

However, what I did not know was that, in reality, I was successful only in my "Job". That's right, I had a $200,000/yr "Job" and that's all. I didn't have a business at all! If I got hurt, sick, or something else, there was nobody, no system, and no redundancies to do my "Job" and my income would come to a screeching halt immediately. They taught me that having a "Job" as an individual in this industry is no way to live and prosper for the long term (which is also the entire point of Michael Gerber's book *The E-Myth*).

I attended all of the conferences with the Craig Proctor program as well as watched all of their webinars. I used their chat room to ask questions and I made a lot of friends in the group. However, I am the type of person that needs to "touch and do things" to actually understand them. It's my personality – it's the way I learn. Maybe you are the same.

Given that, I started traveling. My wife, Jessica, and I drove and flew to the offices of the most successful people in the Craig Proctor organization and literally sat in their offices for 1 to 3 days each learning their systems. We visited Jay Macklin in Scottsdale, Lester Cox in Tempe, Wally Kerr in Oklahoma, as well as Francois Mackay and Francis Lavoie in Montreal, Canada to name a few. I also had a 20 minute life-changing phone conversation with Tim Johnson from Florida (Tim was also a Marine). Did you ever think that somebody could change your life in 20 minutes over the phone? Tim did just that for me and I will be forever grateful.

Each of these people is a multi-million dollar per year producer. In their offices I learned where their leads came from, how they captured them, who spoke to them, what they said, how they nurtured them, how they were handed to the Agents, what the agents did and said to them, how they closed them, and even how everybody was paid for their jobs amongst many other things. Basically, I learned each of their systems inside and out.

Those trips were absolutely invaluable as they provided me the opportunity to see first-hand exactly how the most successful companies in North America conducted business and exactly what it was that made them so successful.

After those visits, I both had the template for success AND had seen the template in action. All that was needed was organizing and implementing the systems I had learned.

Organization:

Often times this is the hardest part for people. Especially with the business model that the Proctor program teaches. It's vastly different than any other real estate business model out there and there are seemingly a million moving parts (which there are not, it just seems that way at first). The good news is that you can use just portions of it (which will provide success) or you can implement the whole thing (for massive success). The question of "Where do I start?" becomes the pertinent question. That's where organizational skills come to play. For those that can multi-task and prioritize, its actually easier than you may think.

At my first Proctor conference, I took 26 pages of hand written notes (single spaced on a legal tablet). Holy Cow!!! That's a lot! It was all so new . . . But SO GOOD! How could anybody possibly do it all? How could anybody actually figure out where to start?

The answer actually was pretty simple . . . once I figured out the trick. To cope with the massive number of things I had to do to implement the systems, I simply opened an Excel spreadsheet and created columns across the top that read like this: Person, Priority, Task. That's it, just three simple columns.

Person: Whose job is it to complete this task

Priority: On a scale of 1 to 10 – how important is it that this job get done

Task: A brief description of what it is that needs to be done

The next step is to sort and filter it in the order that I need it to be displayed (there is a "Sort & Filter" tab on the Excel tool bar. I simply sorted by Name, then Priority). The result was the tasks sorted by the person's name (A to Z), then sorted by priority of that task (10 to 1). So when the list was complete, all anybody had to do was scroll to their name and their tasks were in order from highest priority (those with 10's) down to those with the lowest priority (those with 1's). It looks like this:

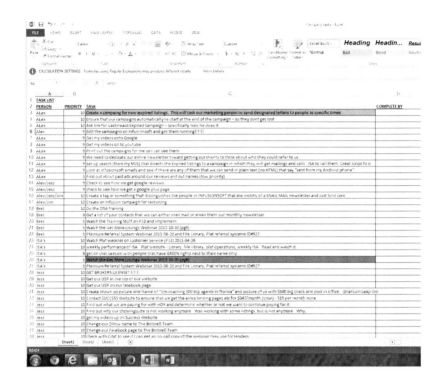

This little excel spreadsheet ensured that I and my staff stayed on track and did the things that needed to be done, in the order that they needed to be done. It was a simple little trick that helped us grow our company by a factor of 5 in just over 2 years.

Interesting and important note: This list is <u>NEVER DONE</u>. I have found that I am <u>always</u> adding to it . . . always tweaking and improving the systems. Given that, it's best to consider it a "living document".

Systems:

I am a big fan of systems . . . as you might imagine from my long experience in the Marine Corps.

Once I started implementing the systems that my coaches were showing me, I noticed an immediate change in my business. First of all, it made Real Estate fun again! Secondly, it became immensely more profitable AND . . . I didn't have to do all of the work myself. As Michael Gerber says in his book *The E-Myth* – I was in a rut of "doing it, doing it, doing it". Once Craig and Todd showed me how I could get away from that, life took a wonderful turn.

Now we have automated systems that obtain large quantities of leads each month, Inside Sales Agents (ISA's) that grab and nurture those leads until they are ready to buy or sell, Outside Sales Agents that help the client buy or sell a home using scripts and presentations that are provided to them. Everybody knows exactly where they are in the system (I make sure they understand the bigger picture) and what their responsibilities to the system are. The truly spectacular part of the system is that it repeats itself over and over each month. My Outside Sales Agents are not bogged down with the marketing it takes to get buyers and sellers, the nurturing of their pipeline, or the mounds of paperwork associated with real estate transactions. They can focus on their clients and selling homes. They love it!

My job, as the owner, was to create and implement the systems. The systems now run the company. Today I manage the systems by overseeing them and constantly tweaking and improving them to make them more efficient (hence, the task list is never complete). I am very lucky that my coaches provided working templates and people that I could consult with any time I had a question.

What Makes Us Better:

Are we better than the vast majority of real estate companies? Absolutely we are. Are my Agents better than the vast majority of Real Estate Agents out there? Absolutely they are! You might ask yourself why . . .:

First of all, we have the best training in the world. While my Agents receive the same training that every other real estate company provides (what Escrow does, how Title works, how to properly write contracts, etc., etc., etc.), my agents also get trained on how to SELL, NEGOTIATE and how to TALK TO PEOPLE! That's right, as weird as it may seem, other companies do not train agents how to sell, negotiate, or even how to talk to people. For the life of me I don't understand why - but they don't. I always say, "That's great that (agency) taught you how to fill out a purchase contract . . . but if you have no idea how to sell, you will never see one."

The other thing that makes us better is that we provide VALUE to our clients. That's right, VALUE. We have proprietary systems that other companies simply don't have. For Buyers, we have access to not-yet-on-the-market listings that other companies simply don't have among other things. Further, we retain our Buyer leads through our "Buyer Satisfaction Guarantees" and other Unique Selling Propositions (USP's) that other companies don't provide to their Buyers. We don't lose buyers to outside agents – it just doesn't happen.

For our Sellers, we have cutting edge technology that helps us sell their homes much quicker and for more money than our competitors do. We have found it very simple to win nearly every single listing presentation that we go on just by demonstrating our proven systems, our superior statistics, as well as our Seller Satisfaction Guarantees and our other Seller Unique Selling Propositions (USP's).

Overall, we have better systems. We have learned how to capture a large number of Buyer and Seller leads and HOLD ON TO THEM through the use of an Inside Sales Team and systems that nurture those leads until they are ready to buy or sell. Long gone are the days of my agents trying sell homes AND nurture their pipeline as we all know that 90% of those leads will eventually get ignored and those clients end up buying or selling through somebody else. After all, those people ARE going to buy or sell, the only question is whether or not you will be a part of it. Our systems prevent the loss of those leads and my Agents can concentrate on selling homes and making money.

Lastly, I owe a very big THANK YOU to Craig Proctor, Todd Walters, Jay Macklin, Tim Johnson, Wally Kerr and many others for showing me the path to success. All of us at Ardent Real Estate Services thank you.

Jim Bottrell was born in San Pedro California on October 15th, 1970. His father was a Marine who later became a police officer, his mother a nurse. A salt-of-the-earth, hard working middle-class blue collar family.

Growing up, Jim played lots of sports. Mostly football and baseball where he was routinely on whatever all-star team there was. He was the kid that got to practice early and stayed late in order to be the best. However, he was not one to ever trash talk and was the first to congratulate an opponent that truly beat him at the game. Then he practiced harder to ensure that it would never happen again.

In high school, Jim started his own business washing cars. The business developed into a full-blown auto detailing "business" by the time he was 19 and he used his earnings to put himself through college . . . debt free. He sold his business the day he graduated from college and went into the mortgage lending industry. At just 21, he found it difficult for people to take him seriously so he learned some tricks to take peoples mind off of how young he was. One such trick was the ability to write and do math upside down. Try it . . . Jim would sit across from clients and write out mortgage closing costs, payments, whatever he needed to write out – all upside down. It was a very profitable "trick".

However, mortgage was not where is heart was. By the age of 22 he was a private pilot. A skill that he took to very rapidly and easily. But Jim wanted more – he wanted to fly military jets.

At the age of 23 he visited several military recruiters to inquire about flight opportunities. Jim wanted to follow in his father's footsteps and become a Marine. However, becoming a Marine Corps Officer was something that proved to be much more difficult than he expected . . . and they were not offering Flight Contracts. The selection process to become an officer in the Marine Corps was an extremely difficult one. Only 1% of applicants get an opportunity to go to Officer Candidates School (which, in itself, has an attrition rate of over 50%). Jim was not selected on his first attempt. Nor was he selected on his second attempt. Nor was he selected on his third attempt. Each time, Jim improved his package, worked harder, and he was eventually selected on his 4th attempt. Although he was not offered a "flight contract", Jim went into the Marine Corps in hopes of being a pilot . . . just getting there "the hard way".

Jim suffered tremendously through the grueling Marine Corps Officer Candidates School (OCS). The arches in his feet collapsed, he suffered ACL and MCL injuries, a gastro-intestinal virus, and a consistent sickness often referred to as "the crud". At one point Jim was offered an opportunity to go home, heal up, and come back but he refused. Not so much out of honor or something like that, he simply said, "No, I'm not doing this again. I finish this now!"

After being one of the 43% that graduated from his OCS class, Jim entered the Fleet Marine Force as a Platoon Commander in 2nd Battalion, 4th Marines (called 2/4). In his 3 years with 2/4, Jim did multiple deployments and also spent a lot of time shooting competitively for the Marine Corps in national rifle and pistol matches. He earned multiple medals in both types of weapons.

Jim then went on to become a Company Commander at MCRD San Diego – Marine Corps Boot Camp. There he led over 800 recruits, 32 Drill Instructors, and his company staff through 9 recruit training cycles. He says that tour was his absolute favorite time in his 10 years as an active duty Marine and he says he would drop everything and go back and do it again tomorrow if the opportunity presented itself.

During that tour, the events of 9-11 changed the world. Like all Marines, Jim wanted some payback as did all Americans so he relished his opportunity to go back to the infantry and deploy to Iraq. Jim was assigned as a Company Commander once again.

In the first night of the invasion, Jim's company of 255 Marines successfully took an Iraqi military air base 50 miles deep into Iraq. At dawn of the first morning of the war, that air base became the main logistics hub for the Marine Corps. Soon after, he led his company into the city of Nasariyah where he and his Marines experienced the multi-dimensional art of fighting inside of a city. He now says, "You only really appreciate life once somebody has tried to take it from you." Jim says his greatest accomplishment in life was that all of his Marines came home from the war, back to their

families, with all of their fingers and toes intact. An accomplishment that he relishes every day.

After returning from the war, Jim was promoted to Major where he became a Battalion Operations Officer, which put him 3rd in command of over 1,800 Marines. But he discovered that he preferred being a Captain, "out in the field WITH MY MARINES vs. sitting at this stupid desk". In late 2004, Jim moved on from his career in the Marine Corps and started his civilian life.

For a couple of years, he "flipped" houses. Made good money but it was a tough life. In late 2006, it was obvious that owning extra properties would soon become a money losing endeavor so he stopped flipping houses and used the skills that he learned buying and selling his own homes by helping others own or sell their homes. Yes, as unlikely as it sounds, Jim became a real estate agent.

Real Estate:

When he was a new agent with Realty Experts, he hit the ground running and achieved an impressive sales record putting him consistently in the top two agents in an office of over 180 agents.

After 4 more years working under a broker, Jim decided to venture out on his own and create his own company. That company is Ardent Real Estate Services.

If the highest form of flattery is imitation, Jim has paid lots of compliments over the course of his career. Not one to reinvent the wheel, he firmly believes that the best way to be successful is to follow in the footsteps of those who already are. So when he opened his brokerage in late 2012, he decided to pattern his practices after Craig Proctor and Todd Walters. The two of them have achieved something that only a handful of people have in history and that's to sell over a BILLION dollars of real estate. Yes . . . with a "B". Through a tremendous amount of very hard work, he learned how to implement systems that Craig and Todd used to be so successful.

On the surface, most people probably would not have expected him to be in any sort of coaching program because he is an extreme "Type-A" personality. With his large amount of personal experience with real estate having been a Mortgage Lender, a General Contractor, and having his own personal rental properties, some would say that he already possessed everything he needed to be successful. Truth be told – he was "successful". But, once he joined the Proctor program he learned that there were many definitions of the word "successful".

After two hard years of building and implementing the Proctor systems, "The Bottrell Team" is now in the top 1% in homes sold in Southern California and has just earned its 4th consecutive 5-star award for premier customer satisfaction. An award presented by San Diego Magazine to just a few agents each year.

Furthermore, The Bottrell Team was recently recognized as one of the top 200 most respected real estate teams in all of North America and was presented the "Quantum Leap Award" in 2013, an award presented by Craig Proctor himself to the agent or team that demonstrates the highest rate of growth in his program.

Jim was also invited to be part of Craig Proctor's inner circle that he calls "Titanium". This is a small group of just 20 hand-selected people to be part of his personal mentoring and business development program. This group is made up of only the very top agents in North America. Jim still wonders how he ever got an invitation to this group but he knew that selection to this elite group is about as big an advantage as anybody can have.

Success:

Organization and efficiency has propelled Jim's company to grow exponentially over the 24 months since joining the Proctor program. Before Jim started with the program, he typically sold about 25 homes per year with an annual commission income of approximately $210,000. Most people would think that is pretty good. Many would call it "successful". So did Jim . . . until he met some truly astounding people in the Proctor program that showed him a different way of working and a different way of thinking. Since that fateful introduction into the program in January 2013, his commission revenues have doubled and then doubled again. Yes, it's true - he went from $210,000 in gross revenue from 23 sales in 2012 to $434,000 from 40 sales in 2013 then to an astounding $885,000 from 72 sales in 2014. Furthermore, as of this writing on January 21, 2015 – He currently has over $250,000 in commission revenue from 26 sales in escrow right now! That's in January – a month where most agents are still on vacation and thinking about maybe going back to work sometime after the super bowl.

Jim set his 2015 goals to earn $1,500,000 and close 120 transactions in the year. Given that he is only 21 days into the year and already has 26 sides and over $250,000 commission income in escrow . . . He is looking to revise his goals upward.

Jim attributes his success to three things: 1. His experience from the Proctor program, 2. His ability to implement and lead people to a common goal and 3. His superior support staff and real estate agents.

Jim hires mostly Marines. 80% of his agents are Marines and his entire company staff was sourced from Wounded Warrior Battalion. Wounded

Warrior Battalion is comprised of Marines that have been wounded in combat to the point where they can no longer serve in an Active Duty role. He admires these individuals not just for what they have overcome, but because they have a Can-Do attitude. Jim calls them "fire and forget" missiles- by that he means that he simply gives them a task to accomplish (what in the Marine Corps is called his "Final Result Desired") and they do whatever it takes to get it done with very little follow up or supervision necessary.

Moving Forward:

Success is a relative term. People view it differently as their perspectives and expectations of success are different. Jim has considered himself successful many times in his life only to find that "the bar" has been moved. Sometimes from an external experience, sometimes self-generated.

The point being that you are never "done". You are either implementing, growing, and building or you are fading and dying. Which one are you?

Chapter 11
Celebrity Brand

by Marnie Bennett

How to Position Yourself as the Expert, Authority, Even Celebrity Agent in Your Market for Complete Annihilation of Your Competition

These days, we all understand the importance of branding ourselves, of connecting our names to a compelling identity in order to attract clients. The meatier challenge can be finding an effective medium through which to market our brands – preferably, a medium that isn't already flooded with competitors.

From my humble beginnings to the present day, I've pursued many different avenues to "get my name out there". And I'd have to say that the most unusual and successful tactic I've employed is hosting my own radio show.

The goals were to increase my name and brand recognition, and to solidify my reputation as a real estate educator and mentor. Those goals have definitely been met. But very quickly, somewhat to my surprise, I also became a popular radio personality with a devoted following. Five years after making the leap, I can say that the majority of my firm's clients come to us as a direct result of our radio presence.

When I was starting out in real estate, I never dreamed of becoming a radio celebrity. But today, I've come to genuinely love the medium. While radio and television are both terrific ways to reach the public, there are a couple of obvious advantages to radio. It's generally easier to break into, and it's less expensive to produce and air. Radio also offers a warmth that television lacks.

Well-known journalist Peggy Noonan perfectly expressed the subtle power of radio when she wrote, "TV gives everyone an image, but radio gives birth to a million images in a million brains." Radio actively engages our imaginations. It lends itself to a more intimate relationship between speaker and listener; when we listen, it's easy to imagine that the speaker is in direct conversation with us. I've had more people than I can count tell me, "I felt like I already know you." Less glitzy than TV, radio is a perfect tool for establishing real estate professionals as real, approachable people with legitimate expertise to share.

I didn't stumble into this gig. I researched the marketing approaches of the top ten realtors in my city; I made an honest assessment of where my own strengths lay; and I made a strategic decision. I'd always been a skilled communicator, and I felt confident that my educational background in law and economics gave me special insight into the real estate market. It seemed that radio might be a great way to showcase these strengths.

I took note of one successful local realtor who had his own radio show. It consisted largely of jokes and name-calling, and seemed to have no purpose or planning. It might as well have aired live from a boys' locker room.

I knew I could do better than that. My concept was essentially the polar opposite: I strove to incorporate elements of informative TV talk shows like Good Morning America and topical news shows like 60 Minutes. Each one-hour show would have its own theme and would be strictly structured with four distinct segments. I planned to invite expert guests to chat with me, and to field calls from listeners.

I approached the radio station with a detailed template, and they were receptive. Next, I began drumming up corporate sponsors – a task that, fortunately, didn't intimidate me. I'd established a good network of business connections over the years, and I had faith in my vision. I commissioned a memorable jingle and, before long, I was hosting a live hour of radio once a week.

While the medium was new to me, I didn't feel I was in completely foreign territory. In the past, I'd worked as a sessional college professor teaching business strategies and marketing. I'd found that the students enjoyed my down-to-earth treatment of the subject matter, particularly my habit of relating various business situations to personal life experiences.

Viewing my classes as a focus group of sorts, I decided to use my teaching style as the basis of my approach to radio.

Our listening audience tends to be well-educated, and includes many entrepreneurs and senior management types; we also have a growing market of ambitious Generation Y listeners. Substance matters to these people. I consider it my mandate to provide information and interpret data in a way that's as far from dull as possible.

Preparation for each show is both time-consuming and vital. Whether the week's topic is women in real estate, first-time buyers, divorce and the division of property, or real estate investment, I'm well-armed with both facts and anecdotes. I spend time researching the global, national and local economies, to ensure my grounding is sound and to give my listeners a broader understanding of the factors at play in the real estate market.

Each week, to encourage audience participation (which increases the likelihood of attracting new clients), we issue an invitation to register online for a workshop, seminar or special event, or offer the chance to become a "VIP Buyer". We also feature online contests. By encouraging a direct response from our listeners, we're also able to size up audience engagement.

Not surprisingly, my biggest challenge has been to keep the show feeling fresh over the years. My original competitor in radio has begun to mimic my style, ideas and information; while imitation is the sincerest form of flattery, this has presented me with an even greater challenge in terms of setting my show apart.

The solution? I never let myself get too comfortable. I push myself to learn new information, new approaches, new technologies. I also switch things up regularly. Sometimes, we air live from outside venues – the sales centre for a new luxury downtown condo, for example. In addition to bringing both local and international real estate and investment experts on the show, I'll feature preferred partners and different members of my team. Every guest has a different area of expertise, different frames of reference and a different personality. That makes for interesting dynamics. As charismatic as you may be, there's no doubt that variety adds both substance and pizzazz.

For those of you who wonder if radio might be the right move for you, I'd suggest you ask yourself if you possess the following qualities:

- Confidence and a comfortable, friendly demeanor. I'm a natural extrovert who loves good conversation. These traits are common to many of us in real estate, and they're essential for radio.

- A warm, listenable voice.
- The self-discipline to be well-prepared every week.
- The ability to think on your feet.
- A talent for breaking down complicated ideas and lingo into easily digested chunks. Let's be honest: real estate figures aren't the stuff Tom Clancy novels are made of. It's up to you to put an interesting spin on them.
- A unique approach. Embrace what makes you different from your competitors. Different sells.
- Tough skin. Those of us who put ourselves in the public eye and achieve recognizable success can attract criticism along with the praise. It can sting; but if you've got faith in yourself, you'll do fine.
- A risk-taking nature. You've got to be willing to push yourself out of your comfort zone, both emotionally and financially. To get big, you've got to embrace the role.
- For those who have the right stuff, a regularly aired radio program provides incredible long-term exposure. Each time you answer a listener's question or interpret the latest housing numbers, you're earning respect and nailing down your reputation more firmly.

And consider these benefits:

- For the client, there's an emotional payoff to having a radio personality as an agent. They feel they're in the best hands; they feel special. They have confidence in you from the get-go. Now it's just up to you to justify that confidence.
- A self-perpetuating cycle is now in place. Because your name is well-known, your clients are more likely to talk about you to others, further increasing your brand presence. People who might have thought *"She's too busy to talk to me"* will realize that you (or one of your team) can, in fact, take them on as clients.
- Radio gives you an instant platform to promote any new venture you embark on. If you're starting a new investors' program, you can publicize it; if you win an award, you can chat about it; if you're running a workshop, you can allude to it. Having said that, it's important to market yourself with class and restraint. If you're skilled, you can work in references to your projects in such a way that they seem natural and helpful.

- Thanks to the internet, radio broadcasts are no longer fleeting. You can give them staying power by posting links to podcasts on your website, together with a summary of the topics covered that week.

Radio isn't for everyone. To make it work, you've got to be willing to make sacrifices – of time, privacy and, initially, money. But trust me on this: when it's done well, it can be a game changer.

Marnie Bennett:

Broker, Real Estate Guru, Mentor & Public Personality

In the sometimes hard-nosed world of real estate, it's a joy to work with a gifted practitioner who believes that business sense and a generous spirit can go hand-in-hand. Marnie Bennett is an educator, mentor and wealth coach to clients who seek to master the art of the wise real estate transaction.

As broker, founder, and shining-star of the Bennett Property Shop Realty, Marnie Bennett has built a one-of-a-kind boutique real estate brokerage in Ottawa, Canada, whose business philosophy is based on exceptional personal service, leadership, industry-leading innovative policies, and practices. Marnie trains a team of 25 elite sales representatives, sharing her remarkable expertise with warmth, humour and outstanding results. The Bennett Property Shop Realty sales volume speaks for itself with over 9,000 homes sold for top dollar since 1994 and over $3.1 Billion in residential sales.

Along the way, she's gathered a devoted following. Always comfortable in the public eye, Marnie has cultivated a strong identity as a print columnist, radio personality and internationally recognized public speaker. Such engagements allow her to share her knowledge with a wide audience base, including first-time homebuyers, budding entrepreneurs and high-ranking executives. Marnie is considered among the legal profession to be the leading expert witness for condominiums.

Passionate about her calling and deeply dedicated to her clients,
Marnie Bennett doesn't
hesitate when asked
about her multi-faceted
career as mentor, marketer,
broker and public figure.

"Some people feel
boxed-in by their professions,
with no room to breathe. I've
never felt that way," she says.
"I've shaped my career in a
way that allows me to explore
my strengths – one of which
is connecting with people. If there's a chance for me to share what I know
with others, I'll jump at it."

"For me, this is the best job in the world," Marnie says simply; and
we'd have to agree.

In the Limelight

Marnie's substantial media presence sees her frequently sharing her
knowledge in public forums. On television, she has been recruited by
CTV News for commentary as a real estate expert, and by CBC News
as an expert on the condo market. In print, she has written a nationally
syndicated column, *Property Talk*, for CanWest Global newspapers, while
her *Home Smarts* column appears regularly in New Home and Condo
Guide magazine. And in radio, Marnie appears on the weekly show –
Experts on Call - The Real Estate Edge aired by Bell Media stations.

International Presence

In addition to her high profile in Canada, Marnie has become a
popular speaker at conferences and workshops in the US and has received
a number of international real estate awards including the prestigious
"Daniel Passante Entrepreneurship Award" and the "Top Dog Award"
from Craig Proctor Real Estate Systems in recognition as being the best
and most productive agent in North America. With extensive knowledge
of the American real estate market and a large network of international
contacts, Marnie is well-positioned to advise on transactions abroad, as
well as at home.

Mentoring and Education

An ardent educator, Marnie uses many avenues to reach people at different stages of their personal financial journeys. Aspiring and established real estate investors are able to engage with her in intense, one-on-one mentoring sessions. As a wealth coach, she works closely with clients to design and execute custom-made plans of action. And for those dipping their toes in the waters for the first time, Marnie is continually creating educational opportunities that are fun, practical and easily understood.

Since 2008, Marnie has been educating the general public through a series of free specialty seminars called "Learn How to Increase Your Wealth Through Real Estate".

As a self-made businesswoman who, as a child, witnessed the financial struggles of her single mother, Marnie is particularly passionate about helping other women discover their aptitudes for business, investment and entrepreneurship. To this end, she's developed the "WOW [Women on Wealth] Workshops," aimed specifically at the female demographic. In addition to inviting highly respected real estate analysts and experts to speak frankly to "ladies only" audiences, Marnie has added a component of informative entertainment in the form of "Invest and Dress for Success" fashion shows.

In 2012 Marnie hosted and created a unique entrepreneurial weekly hourly radio show with Bell Media called "*Business Class*". This educational business show helped to guide small businesses to their road to success.

In recognition of her extraordinary teaching skills and business expertise, Marnie was recruited by Algonquin College to become a faculty member in the Business Department, teaching "Success Strategies" to young entrepreneurs.

Super-Marketing

Marnie has long been considered the "go-to gal" for condo and home developers who seek stand-out marketing strategies. Her reputation as a marketing dynamo is well-earned: to each new project, she brings a stream of stimulating ideas, together with the high-placed connections necessary to make those ideas come to life. In the 1990s, Marnie honed her skills during her tenure as Executive Vice-President of a highly successful custom home builder; as the company grew to gross in excess of $40,000,000 annually under her leadership, she became known as a fearless innovator of cutting-edge marketing approaches.

Recognition in the Field

Marnie's extraordinary accomplishments have been recognized both within her home city and on the international playing field. Marnie has won over 20 marketing awards for innovative marketing strategies and creative advertising in the housing industry. In 2008, Marnie was named Ottawa's Professional Businesswoman of the Year. In 2010, she was named the #1 Broker Worldwide for Keller Williams Realty International. She was the first woman to receive this high distinction. More recently, Bennett Real Estate Professionals won the 2011 Better Business Bureau Torch Award in the Professional Service category for Exceptional Customer Service and Marketplace Trust. Again in 2011, Marnie was named #1 Broker Worldwide for Keller Williams Realty International.

Public Roles & Philanthropy

Over the course of her consistently demanding career, Marnie has given her time to serve on the Board of Directors for the Ottawa Congress Centre as Marketing Director; as Director of the Ottawa Board of Trade; and as appointee to the Mayor's taskforce on affordable housing.

On a personal level, Marnie's love of athletics and national pride has spurred her to take an active role in the sponsorship of Olympic hopefuls. She and her family are also long-time supporters of young Canadian soccer and hockey players, billeting members of the Ottawa 67's and working for a renewal of soccer fields throughout Ottawa. "When you see these young athletes, they're full of fire and hope," she says. "It's truly inspiring." Spoken like a true mentor.

Marnie can be reached at 613-233-8606 or marniebennett@ bennettpros.com or www.bennettpros.com

Chapter 12
Building a Winning Team: Always Be Recruiting

by Wally Kerr

I'm a HUGE Oklahoma City Thunder fan. Though I'm an avid sports fan and MC for the University of Oklahoma on home football game days, I never really cared about the NBA until the Thunder and Kevin Durant came to town. Now, I rarely miss a game on TV, and attend many when they play at home. The tandem of Durant and Russell Westbrook is amazing to watch, along with an amazing supporting cast. Like any other successful team, the composition of today's Thunder basketball team was built one player at a time, and the draft picks and subsequent player trades over the last three to five years have finally assembled a group of superstars who seem to "really" enjoy playing and competing together. The Thunder team analyzes its needs, and then drafts or trades for new players each season in hopes of building the best possible team. Each player has their own strengths, with each contributing to the team in their own unique way.

In the 2014 Western Conference Playoffs, the Thunder were beat out of the finals by San Antonio, who ultimately went on to the finals and defeated the Miami Heat for the 2014 NBA Title. Though OKC swept the Spurs 4-0 in the regular season, the Spurs found a way to beat OKC at its own game in the playoffs. Greg Popovich has now won 5 NBA Championships as the Spurs Coach, and all since 1999. Again this year, the Spurs were credited as a team that played with great humility, passing the ball on offense with lightning speed until a player had a "great" shot at the basket. These are professional players making millions per season . . . . . . true SUPERSTARS; the Best of the Best. They understand teamwork and success at a level much greater than most of us will ever experience; knowing that just one or two additional losses in the regular season makes all the difference in having a home-court advantage when it's time for the Playoffs. More important, it's been said that no matter which Spurs player is substituted into a game, it has little effect on the game outcome. Each player CLEARLY understands his role in the game . . . his strengths and weaknesses, and the reason he was drafted and signed (or traded) to the Spurs, and how his play specifically influences the outcome of the game.

Todd Walters, our Platinum coach in Craig Proctor's Platinum Program, often references the Atlanta Braves, and their constant recruiting efforts to continually replace their "worst player." In our business careers, most of us have heard the term "your business is only as good as your weakest employee." Thus, the Braves, the Thunder, the Spurs and every other professional sports franchise recruits, drafts or trades to replace its "weakest link." Recruiting NEVER stops. Within the Craig Proctor organization, we refer to it as "ABR"----Always Be Recruiting.

I see my real estate team today, their skills and productivity, and realize that I've recruited and built my real estate team much like the Thunder, Spurs and Braves have done. Each member of my team was recruited for their individual skills . . . . . . specifically, the members of my administrative team, though I've also recruiting specific agents to fill "gaps" in working with certain buyer and seller personalities. I'll get to that more in a moment. Specifically, I don't need my staff closing coordinator or customer service representative to have great sales skills. If they did, they'd ask to join the sales team and could make the money that some of my top agents make, though they would give up a predictable 8-430pm weekday

job and regular paycheck. Instead, these very "detailed" personalities are the glue that holds my office together. Unlike my highest earning salespeople, they strive for a neat and organized desk at the end of each day. They collect the paperwork that literally flies around in the office, pulling each sheet out of the air, organizing and filing the details that the busiest agents produce. I've made that sound more dramatic than it is; as we went paperless nearly two years ago with online document management (we use SKYSLOPE.) Still, the highest producing agents in my office take longer to complete their files, which must be done for them to be paid after closing. My customer service manager CLEARLY understands her role in our machine. As the market has improved and become red-hot in many price ranges in 2014, listings are "priceless." A home priced right in our market is going to sell. With my agents as busy as ever, these listings must be serviced and protected. My customer service manager understands how important it is that these home sellers hear from someone in my office regularly. Our policy is once a week, minimum, though every home seller will tell you how often they'd like to hear from you . . . . . . just ask . . .! We've all had home sellers who are so laid back that they say "call me when you get an offer!" Others need daily attention, or to hear from us two or three times a week. As far as I'm concerned, that better be a really GREAT listing to earn that kind of attention, right? Simply put, real estate is a service business, and keeping the customer informed and happy is #1 in our firm. My customer service rep was easy to find . . . she'd been in the customer service field previously. My staff closing coordinator was easy to find, too . . . she was previously a vice-president at a local credit union, but wanted to work for a smaller, more personal firm with fewer headaches and red-tape.

My recruiting and hiring is no different than with the OKC Thunder. When the Thunder realized it needed more offense and scoring late this season—when it was clear they would make the 2014 Playoffs, they brought in free agent Caron Butler, an 11 year veteran who had a great jump-shot outside the paint, but could also hit the three point shot with 40% accuracy. First, the Thunder identified its need, and then recruited accordingly. Why should your business be any different? What is it that your business needs now to take its next step forward? In my case, and prior to hiring my staff closing coordinator, my top agent might sell seven homes in March, but only 2 more in April. Obviously, he was consumed with the activities it took to get those seven homes he sold in March to the closing table. If his forte is selling, why should he be doing ANYTHING other than selling? Are you so busy that you can no longer call each of your sellers every week? What will happen if this continues to occur and you lose touch? This became an issue for me as we grew quickly . . . . . . I had more listing calls and home sellers than I could keep up with. If you lost just ONE listing every other month over the next year due to poor communication, what would the cost to you be at the end of the year?

It probably comes as no surprise that superstars like Kevin Durant, LeBron James and Peyton Manning actually have "coaches" themselves. They are the most talented athletes in the world at their own positions, yet they are humble enough to accept training and coaching from others to become an even BETTER player. I needed this lesson in humility. As I grew more successful, I became LESS willing to learn from others . . . as I became the "superstar" in my local market. From 2002 to 2006, working only with my wife, one admin assistant and a new agent I had hired (who is now my top producing agent), I was closing 60-65 homes per year on my own, and my wife was doing very little selling. Mostly, she assisted in the office and managed our personal lives, family and finances, as I was seldom home. I started each day around 8:30am, and worked most weekdays until 8 or 9pm, regularly giving listing presentations AFTER others had fed THEIR families and were finally ready to meet with me to discuss the sale of their home. My income was stable, but not increasing during that five year period . . . stuck on earnings of $375,000 to $425,000 per year. My mind was closed to doing business a different way, and I was becoming burned out.

Headed into the spring market in 2007, I remember sitting at my office desk, lamenting how much time, energy and effort it would take to churn out another $400,000 in income . . . perhaps a little more . . . in the spring and summer months. I had worked myself to death, prospecting constantly and competing fiercely with several other local agents who were "hot on my tail." I was #1 in my market in closed sales volume in 2004, 2005 and 2006, but I wondered if I'd be able to hold up to pull it off again in 2007. I had closed 62 homes in 2006, with closed volume at just above $13,000,000. In the back of the March issue of REALTOR magazine was a picture of Craig Proctor with several medals pulling his head to the floor, being rewarded by Dave Liniger as the #2 RE/MAX agent worldwide. I even remember the headline at the top . . . I can see the words clearly in my mind, even today . . . "I work 40 hours a week and made $1.5M last year." I remember thinking "BS . . . that can't be true. I work much harder than that and don't make anywhere near that. He must be in Hollywood and have an average sales price of $9,000,000. He probably sells all the movie-stars' homes."

I called the toll free number and was connected to his coaching office. I was told that his statements were true, that an upcoming conference in Dallas was near my location, and was also assured that I could sit in the SuperConference until noon on the second day and still receive a full refund of my tuition if I didn't feel the ideas that had already been shared by that time would allow me to earn an extra $50,000 in income that year, if implemented.

Truth was, Craig was in a small town outside Toronto, Canada, and his average sales price was near $300,000. He was closing about 550 homes per year, and was a dedicated agent much like me. Craig was humble on stage as he recited his background and upbringing, the son of a real estate broker. Craig saw things differently. What I learned from Craig would change my paradigm and career.

Wally Kerr began his real estate career in 1987, at the persuasion of an old friend who owned a Better Homes and Gardens real estate franchise. Wally owned a popular mobile disc-jockey company called Mobile Music Unlimited, and also DJed on his off nights at several local nightclubs, always struggling to stay ahead financially. In 1992, Kerr was offered the broker position and a minority ownership in the Better Homes and Gardens franchise, until it was closed in 1992 and he and his wife Cindy moved to RE/ MAX in Norman, Oklahoma. They remained with that same firm until March 2010, when they opened their first office, Kerr Team Real Estate. Kerr has now been Norman's top ranked residential agent by either sales volume or number of closed transactions every year since 2007, and as of the publication date of this book, Kerr has remained at the top in Norman through 2014. He and Cindy have two offices and a plan to open a 3rd, with over $92,000,000 in sales in 2014 and an average of just over 40 homes sold per agent in both 2013 and 2014.

Chapter 13
Shortcut to Success

by Debbie Renna-Hynes & Todd Walters

Successful People Are Willing To Do Things Unsuccessful People Aren't

I don't think it's a big secret or even a little secret that super successful people do things that the majority simply are not willing to do, or do not want to do.

My story is well documented. At a young age, I resolved to be a Millionaire Agent. Impatient, I sought out the #1 Agent in North America and paid him large sums of money to both show me how to do it and to license me his stuff to copy and use in my market place. That was a good move. I went on to be written about in books, touted as one of the top agents in the U.S. and contracted by arguably the #1 Millionaire Agent Maker Coach in North America to help him coach.

Let's look at it a different way though. Let's say you make clocks and you sell your clocks for $10 each. Business is OK, not great, but OK. You get by. Then your buddy from college comes along and he gets into the same business, making and selling clocks. A year later you read about your buddy in the newspaper, in the business section, as his company has just been named one of the fastest growing clock making companies in the city.

You investigate and find out that he made a deal with Disney to put Mickey Mouse on his clocks and sell them for $50 each. Your response? "Well I could sell more clocks too if I did that . . . !"

But you go back to your clock making business, back to the status quo. Not much changes.

I see this kind of thing happen every day of my year, but with agents and the decisions and choices they make. We talk to agents and offer them opportunity, for a fee, to come and learn from Billion Dollar Agents, hang out with Millionaire to Multi-Millionaire Agents, copy stuff that will bring in more business . . . again for a fee, but most say no. Some though, say yes. You are reading about some of those in this book. ALL say they want to do more, can do more, but only some are willing to actually do things different, like pay for coaching.

I see this as no different than paying for college. Same mind set. No different than Michael Jordan paying for a personal coach, or Tiger Woods paying for a personal coach. I am pretty sure just about every successful person has bartered, traded or paid directly someone MORE successful for their knowledge or stuff so they too could be like them.

Bottom line is you will want to resolve to pay any price, make any sacrifices necessary to quantum leap your business, IF you really want to. This includes coaching. But not just any old coach. Very few have ever made millions of dollars selling real estate. Even fewer taught others how to make millions selling real estate. Even fewer are doing both very successfully and profitably.

Nevertheless, be willing to do things most are not willing to do. Debbie Renna-Hynes comes to mind. I remember the exact moment she joined our Platinum Millionaire Agent Maker Program. In fact I will never forget it. As she got up out of her chair to turn her form in, she tripped and flew across the room. It was quite a scene, but it did not deter her from moving forward. She had resolved to quantum leap her real estate business. And quantum leap she did, flying across the room aside.

Let's hear from Debbie on the matter. **– Todd Walters**

✦ ✦ ✦

It's How Much??!!!

by Debbie Renna-Hynes

I can remember as if it were yesterday. I was walking up one of those crazy hills in Austin, Texas, where I had just attended a real estate conference when I turned to a fellow Real Estate agent and asked, "Where is Stephanie?" My broker said, "She is with her Coach." I said, "Really, she has a Real estate coach? How much does that cost??" I just about fell over when I heard the words "$1000 per month!"

When I entered into the glamorous world of Real Estate, I never dreamed that people had coaches. After all, isn't real estate easy? It's just about buying and selling houses. Anyone can do that right?

WRONG!!!

Throughout history, as far back as the writings go, people have always been coached. From teaching man to hunt, cook, and draw paintings on cave walls. I guess even back then the role of the Teacher or Coach can be simply described as helping someone to learn in order to improve their skills.

I had just finished my 25th year as an educator before I started my new career selling real estate. Teaching all ages from children to adults, I could not figure out why it seemed so foreign to me to have a coach. I went to the dictionary for a true definition and read that a coach or trainer can help one through the development process of a specific area. Coaches help the individual or group achieve specific goals, achievements, stay on task, and make one accountable. And, while it may be in a one-on-one relationship or in a group setting, opportunities are presented and the coach's job is to challenge the learner so they can discover new ways and ideas instead of the "same old, same old, thing."

This makes great sense. As some of the biggest businesses in the world, sports teams have coaches to make them excel in their game performance. Heck, they even have mind coaches to make sure their head is in the game. Pro golfers have coaches, gymnasts have coaches. Just about anyone you can think of that has some type of performance-based career has a coach. I made the decision to now have a coach, too.

I'm on a mission to see if I can find someone who can display the objects and objections to bring someone to their fullest potential at a new level. That someone is me.

So here I am in real estate selling 30-40 homes a year, never being able to break that number. No matter what I did that same number would appear every year. I kept hearing people say, "Work smarter, not harder." While I felt that I was working this way, looking back I would have to say that I probably worked harder, not smarter.

You see, I would ask every agent I talked to about their business but many felt they couldn't share anything with me. They had to keep all to themselves. I would hear things like, "Here is a phone book . . . start calling!!!!" That's when it finally hit me that for the past 25 years that's exactly what I had been doing. COACHING my students.

The hunt began to find the perfect coach. After all, Tiger Woods had several coaches so why can't I.

There were so many "Real Estate" coaches out there all offering ways to get you rich quick! Well I was all about making money but it had to be the right fit.

When looking for a coach I made a list of what I thought my coach would be:

- A motivator and facilitator
- A time block/time management master
- Someone who can ask questions to make me think or take me through the process on another level
- Goal-oriented to track my growth and help me achieve more.
- A good listener
- A constant source of improving what we are doing so that I can develop new ideas or areas to focus on.
- A person who gives feedback and constructive criticism
- Dedicated to giving me the appropriate level of service
- As passionate as I am about real estate and teaching.
- Heres the biggie . . . drum roll please. That they must have sold or sell REAL ESTATE and a lot of it!

As a Realtor, you receive many solicitations from different companies with each one promising they have the best programs with all the systems and models. I knew that if I took this leap of faith and went to the direction of paying what I thought at the time was a huge investment, this person better be great!

After much research, I found the perfect program that not only included coaching, but systems, scripts, and ideas about how to run your business. After all, a business without a plan is like getting into a car going somewhere you have never been before without directions or a GPS.

I anxiously and patiently awaited my calls from my coach. Each call, we would go over successes of the week along with things in business, and personally, for which I am grateful. Of course, going over my numbers were a big part of the conversation, too. We often talked about books that could be read that could help the business, and of course the closing was always about the one thing that I was to focus on until our next call.

The coaching program proved to be a huge success. I soon learned the difference between working "on" versus "in" my business. The need to learn, and to learn more, stuck to my bones. Within a year my numbers doubled, soon after tripled. I went from being an average solo agent to a mega-agent team leader, running one of the most successful real estate teams in the state of New York.

WOW, this really works. In addition to the one-on-one trainings, emailing back and forth when you need a quick question answered, group calls, there is also a bigger piece to this equation. Three to four times a year we get together to mastermind. There are no words to describe the feeling of getting together with agents from all over the world to discuss ideas: what ideas are working and which ones we have tried that need change. Moreover, the word to describe the friendships made with mega agents around the globe is "PRICELESS!"

Debbie Renna-Hynes

Rochester Realtor Debbie Renna-Hynes wows real estate professionals when she travels to various offices in several states to hold office meetings on "How to be a Mega Agent."

Originally from the New York City area, she holds a bachelor's degree in Fine Arts and a Master's in Education and was a former high school teacher for over 25 years. Debbie Renna-Hynes entered into real estate in 2003. Debbie, a local investor of over 35 years in the Rochester, NY Real estate market felt that with the interest she had in real estate combined with education it was a natural move to become a REALTOR. The merging of the two things she's very passionate about led her to a very fast start in the real estate industry. Renna-Hynes attributes her success in the real estate industry not only to hard work but having real estate coaches. "I have always known that education is important in any business." A little over five years ago she started researching coaches in North America and stumbled across Craig Proctor who is a top agent and coach in his field. It was through Craig Proctor and his coaching organization that she met Todd Walters. With the help of her two coaches, she quickly began to be recognized as a top agent in her area.

She is the CEO of "The Renna Hynes Team" with Keller Williams Realty. Year after year, Debbie ranks high in the Keller Williams local, state, and national levels, and has received numerous awards throughout her career to include her most prized accolade, being named REALTOR Associate of the Year 2007, holding a number of designations and ranked as one of the top agents of her Real Estate Board. Her team is also consistently ranked as one of the top teams in New York State by Real Trends.

Recently, Debbie was featured on the cover of Top Agent Magazine for being at the top of her field nationally. Debbie has always been a leader and a teacher. You might often hear Debbie say "I am a passionate people person! I've taught for over 25 years, and loved learning from my students as they learned from me. Buying and selling a home requires the same kind of passion and dedication."

Debbie, while currently training, teaching/coaching with her team, various market centers and coaching clients throughout North America, continues to run an award winning Real Estate Team. Debbie currently resides in Rochester New York where she has been a resident since 1978. She is proud to have raised her three sons in the area with her husband who is also a realtor. When she's not selling real estate or coaching mega agents, she volunteers her time with the Rochester General Hospital TWIG association, veterans outreach Center, just a few among the number of organizations to which she donates her time. She is also happy to be the continued financial sponsor for "Artistic", an art show for autistic children through *Autism Speaks*. In her spare time (HA!), Debbie continues her artistic endeavors by reading both for personal and professional development, writing, cooking and of course painting.

Chapter 14
Creating the Best
Customer Experience

by Laura Petersen & Todd Walters

What Your Clients Actually Prefer

Judy Agent is out showing homes to a buyer who came in from out of town without much notice. Meanwhile, her listing at 123 Main St., a referral from a friend she works out with, has a buyer knocking at their door. The reason the buyer is knocking on the door is because they drove by the house an hour ago and have been trying to reach the listing agent, Judy, but Judy is tied up with the buyer from out of town.

After looking at the 4th house of the day with the out of town buyer, the buyer looks at Judy and says "... we just don't like any of these homes and now we are having second thoughts about even moving to this part of the city. We are going to have to rethink what we are doing here ..."

Judy, disappointed with the out of town buyer packing it in after a long day of looking, gets around to returning some calls on her way to her daughter's Lacrosse game that she is already 30 minutes late for. The Buyer interested in 123 Main St. does not answer. She thinks nothing of it.

While out to dinner later with her daughter and husband, after the Lacrosse game, her cell phone rings and it's her seller at 123 Main St. The seller expresses his disappointment that a buyer who was knocking on their door as they drove up to their house after returning home from the grocery store said they were in town for a couple days and need a house. They had one picked out but before they made the offer, wanted to see the house at 123 Main St. Judy's seller did not let the buyer in, but did tell the buyer Judy, their agent would call them asap.

Judy told the Seller that she had left the buyers a message but had not heard back from them. The next day Judy called the buyer again and this time the buyer answered, but indicated they had made an offer on another house they had seen earlier.

Does this story sound familiar? Most likely you have a similar one. But the real stories are the ones told by the buyers and sellers, not by the agents. The customer's vote is the one that counts. How do you think the two buyers and the 5 sellers in the above story would vote? Yes, there are two buyers and 5 sellers in the above short, simple story. A lot of people were impacted and influenced by Judy Agent and how she does things.

Delivering a unique customer experience is demanded by sellers and buyers in today's market place. Unfortunately, they rarely get it. Unless they are working with a top notch agent with a stellar sales team. You see, with proper leverage, good systems and people in place, a highly profitable sales team, the above story plays out much differently. It's likely the buyer who came in to town on short notice actually was followed up with, over the phone, and "go-to-meeting" online meetings took place well ahead of time. The buyer KNEW how the agent worked and showed up with an appointment and was looking in the part of the city that was the best fit. It's likely that the buyer wanting to see the listing at 123 Main reached someone live on the phone and scheduled an appointment to see the house, where the agent showed up with other homes as well as a buyer benefits presentation and buyer agreement. All of this happened while the team leader drove their kid to the kid's Lacrosse game early, even helped coach the team, never missing a game or practice.

If you are not sold on the fact that a well-trained, systems dependent team with ambitious team leader provides a much better customer experience than a traditional real estate agent, then I am not sure what else I can say here. The above story is common place.

Let's take a look at Laura Petersen, millionaire agent from the Orlando, FL area. Laura is serious about the customer experience. Much more serious than the majority. She is willing to do things that most are not willing to do. I know most agents say they are serious as well, but how can you service all of your clients simultaneously? And provide them with a great experience to boot? Laura knows how. – **Todd Walters**

Creating the best Customer Experience . . .

by Laura Petersen

We have gone through the Industrial and the Service Age. Experts agree that we are now entering the Experience Age. It is not as much what we do, but how people "feel" as a result of doing business with us.

One of the cornerstones of the Craig Proctor system is to provide "WOW" customer service to the people we work with. Providing this "WOW" service to our clients, we stand out! This is evidenced by some of our recent reviews that you can find on Google all with 5 of 5 stars given by the customers. Here are some of our current reviews:

"We have worked with Laura from FrontGate Realty for just about two years. She was truly the solution to all our problems, she made everything easier. We were out of state the whole 2 years we worked with her. She is very knowledgeable, she was always communicating with us. She told us the many pros and cons of different places we looked at that we would have never thought of. She led us to the perfect home."

"Laura went above and beyond our expectations. She recommended different lenders, she even recommended places outside of what I wanted which was really great. She made sure to show us all our options. She evaluated what I was looking for and found the perfect house in the perfect area."

"My experience with Laura was . . . unexpected. I am based out of state. She picked me up from the airport and took me through a tour of the area. She even dropped me off at the hotel. I never expected a realtor would do that for me. It was a very unique experience. I

Meet us at any of the properties or follow us from FrontGate Realty, 660 Celebration Avenue, Ste 110, Celebration, Florida. We leave promptly at 1PM.

ended up buying three properties through her. She has the experience, knowledge, and professionalism every realtor should have."

"I have not seen a better realtor like Laura. She has a professional approach, knowledge of the product/market, her overall attitude. She goes above and beyond to help the customer. I bought 3 properties through her and will continue to use her. Laura is the best!"

The first thing to providing a great customer experience is to practice "The Golden Rule" . . . Treat everyone the way that you would like to be treated. But, in working with the number of clients that we serve on a daily basis, providing this great customer experience cannot be done without systems and that is where the Craig Proctor Program comes in. The "WOW" customer service is what keeps them coming back and referring others. You can provide it to a couple of people, but with systems, you can provide this service to everyone you work with and do it consistently. Craig's systems are full of follow through plans that include a multi-tiered approach to reach, nurture and respond effectively to leave the customer with this good feeling. You are able to leverage yourself through people, systems and technology.

One of the first technologies to implement is a great contact management system. This will remind you when to contact the client, what has happened in the past with the client and customized action plans of the best time to contact in the future. The contact management system keeps you organized, so you can not only keep track, but many times contact the client just before they were going to call you . . . and impress them that you are on top of their dreams and goals in selling or purchasing homes.

Secondly, as your business grows you will leverage yourself through people. Through Craig's systems, you will find position contracts that outline job descriptions. Since everyone is a little different in what they require . . . they may or may not require a little tweaking for the position you are filling. But they give you a head start in getting someone started. In addition to that, there is an abundance of training. With intensive training, both in-house and out-of-house, the people that you have working for, and with you, give the same customer experience. We use The Craig Proctor system for a lot of our training. There are live calls and webinars on specific subjects to help train the people that work with us. We also use the years of archived calls and webinars that are available on almost every subject and pick what is best for each employee. In addition, there are online and live courses that Craig and Todd Walters, Platinum Coach have available to assist in the team training. This provides a great basis for the team member and saves the team leader time in training to provide consistent service to the clients.

Lastly, having systems in place, systems that service the clients and make you look good and keep your work load to a minimum. Systems need to be in place to contact the clients as mentioned above. Systems to follow through with them giving them updates as a buyer or seller. And follow up systems after the sale to keep the relationship for repeat and referral business.

It is not one thing that provides a great customer experience. It is all things together that combine to leave them with a great feeling and that they met their goals. It is ingrained in our corporate culture to provide a great customer experience to each and every client.

Laura Petersen

In 2005, with over 20 years of business management and ownership, Laura started her Real Estate career in Orlando, Florida. In 2008, Laura bought FrontGate Realty and has continued to build a successful Real Estate team and business. Laura and her team sell hundreds of homes and consistently earn a 5 star rating by their clients for their excellent customer service.

Laura is a member of the Platinum Group of the Craig Proctor Quantum Leap System as well as the elite Titanium Group, consisting of agents in the top 1% of North America. In 2014, Orlando Style Magazine named Laura as one of the top 10 Realtors in Orlando. Laura also coaches realtors across North America in the Craig Proctor Quantum Leap System.

Laura grew up in Iowa, and graduated with an Accounting degree from the University of Iowa. She has passed both the CPA and CMA exams. She lived and worked in Chicago for many years before relocating to Orlando. She enjoys traveling, reading by the pool, bike riding and spending time with family and friends. Laura is very involved with various ministries and her church and sits on several boards, both ministry and community.

Chapter 15
New England Mogul

by Nathan Clark & Todd Walters

Ambition is Required

I admit that I am somewhat shielded from agents, and people in general, who lack ambition. Still, on occasion I encounter them. Make no mistake about it, these types are deadly. They will sink your business, either on purpose, or by accident. Or at the very least, keep you/it from doing amazing things. Do all you can to steer clear of those that lack ambition and surround yourself with those that possess it.

I understand that virtually every agent will tell you they want to be more successful. Saying that requires nothing but a voice. BUT . . . doing that requires much, much more.

Ambition would be one such requirement. Ambition to have what a truly, highly profitable real estate sales team will give you. Our Craig Proctor Coaching Programs are packed full of such types.

One such agent that comes to mind when I think of the word "ambition" is Nathan Clark, of Rhode Island. Nathan is an aggressive, serial real estate business builder. When I first met Nathan he was doing well, earning about $300,000 a year from his real estate business. Shortly after joining our Platinum Millionaire Agent Maker Program, he propelled himself to #1 with RE/MAX, in all of New England. I got to watch as he voraciously implemented the systems we make available, growing his real estate business *to well over $1 Million in a very short period of time. What I most like about Nathan is that he tests. He has no issue with investing in marketing, testing and split testing message-to-media-to-market match, pressing his team to track every lead, measuring what works and what does not.*

His story is a good one and worth studying for any ambitious-minded agent. But don't take my word for it. I will let Nathan tell it to you. **– Todd Walters**

✦ ✦ ✦

Rejecting Industry Norms and Standards, Embracing Being Different and Telling That Story

by Nathan Clark

When I first got into this business, I was embarrassed by some of the agents around me. I remember going to a wedding and a fellow real estate agent started passing out business cards to complete strangers. It was like she was getting on her hands and knees and begging for business. I never really bought into this traditional way of getting business.

Doing business this way perpetuates a public view that a real estate agent is not worth much, willing to work 24/7, Sunday's doing open houses, at the beck and call of buyers and sellers. Doing cold calling, saying I'm never too busy for referrals, manipulative closing techniques, and the list goes on and on. I simply do not want a business like that. I want, and work to make my business different. One where prospects seek me out, value my time, my advice, and are willing to pay a premium fee to get me.

But, it's one thing to want a business like this, viewed as an expert, authority, even a celebrity real estate agent, and another thing to actually have one. Wanting one is the first step. The next step is differentiation.

I was starting off in the business at 20 years old and was eager to find out how to be the biggest in the world. It is a lofty goal, I know. I remember going to the local real estate conference and meeting one of the international coaches there. I found him at lunch and I told him my goal of being the number 1 real estate agent . . . in the world. I asked him what I had to do to get there. He looked at me and I think he almost choked on his sandwich. I could tell from that look he thought I was a nut, too ambitious, too lofty a goal. Nonetheless, he was no help, or unwilling to help me.

Make no mistake about it, I am ambitious. I want a super-successful business that helps hundreds of buyers and sellers each year, thousands even. I am impatient to have it. I wake each day with one goal in mind and that is to figure out how to have such a business.

I attended Craig Proctor's Superconference back in 2004, after I learned he was the number 1 RE/MAX Agent in the world. I thought what better way to become #1 than to learn from the #1 agent.

It didn't take long though for my paradigm to change. The way I was thinking about things was keeping me from really achieving amazing things as a Real Estate Agent.

Craig Proctor spoke about a systemized way in which he did things. He showed me that to accomplish more, I must do less. And this is what hooked me. This guy, Craig Proctor, #1 in the world was not just telling me how I should do things, he was actually doing what he was preaching. When he offered to show me how to do more, but by doing less, he had the street credentials to back it up.

Craig spoke the truth about the dogma practices of real estate, how everyone just does what the guy in front of him does, because that's just the way it's been done around here. While other agents and trainer gurus were telling me to meet people on Sundays and ask for referrals and mail out recipe postcards and make cold calls, Craig was telling me to do the opposite.

I learned how to run ads that got prospects calling me vs. me calling them. I learned how to convert these prospects into clients. And I learned how to leverage all of this newfound business to get even more business, to the point where it was way more than I could personally handle.

This overflow of business allowed me to implement Craig's system for recruiting, hiring and training a team. It was at this point where I felt a true real estate business taking shape.

Before I started in Craig Proctor's program I was selling 25 homes a year, doing open houses and working 80 hours per week. I was 20 years old so the hours weren't a problem. What was a problem was living from one closing check to another. It was a continuous roller coaster. You would prospect to find a buyer/seller one week. The next week you would stop prospecting and work on selling the home or finding them a home. The fact that you got paid was great but you were now out of clients because you stopped prospecting so you had to re-start prospecting again and the vicious circle would continue.

One of the first things I copied and implemented from Craig was the performance guarantee, "Your Home Sold or I'll Buy It". I believe this business is full of agents who promise clients the moon and stars to get their business but come up short on meeting the client's expectations. So this performance guarantee was a great way for me to put my money where my mouth was, take all the risk out of selling and Guarantee the Sale of the Sellers Home in under 120 Days, or I would buy it.

Right away this was a home run. I began to advertise this performance guarantee everywhere. We put this message on our business cards, our letterhead, and our signs . . . everywhere I was.

From there we went on to improve our marketing with systems that made it easy for the customer to buy from us. I think this is a big problem in the industry; most consumers don't want to call a salesperson to get information. They just want the information quickly, easily, and with the least amount of hassle. We solved this problem using 24hr real estate information lines and direct response website landing pages.

These unique marketing systems speak to, and about, a prospect's problem. It offers them a FREE report or list of homes that solves their problem. Oh yeah, and there is NO mention of a real estate agent anywhere in this type of marketing. I learned that the more I got in between the prospect and what they wanted, the less calls I got. The more I got out of the way, offering prospects what they wanted without my involvement, the more leads I got.

A good example of this would be:

Distress Sales/Bank Foreclosures.
Get a FREE List of those matching your exact home buying criteria
as often as they become available.
Call 1-800-000-0000 ID 0000 (24Hr Recorded Info).

Another would be:

Free Property Information Packet Available Including:
*Virtual Tour DVD
*Sellers Property Disclosure Statement
*Special Financing Options Available
*Fully Loaded Feature Sheet and More.
Call 800-000-0000 ID 0000 (Talk to no agent).

And another would be

Your Home Sold Guaranteed or I'll Buy It*
Free Report Details the Inner Workings
of This Exclusive Guarantee at www . . . com.

By the time I was 25, I was the number one agent in Rhode Island. We accomplished this by taking the principles taught by Craig and implementing them. In fact, I often heard Todd Walters, Platinum Coach, say that my ability to copy and implement what I learn would directly impact my ability to grow my business. My ability to do that would determine how fast and how profitable my business would become.

As I type this, my systems for direct mail are incredibly profitable. Like the ones we are mailing to expired listings, FSBO's and Old Cancelleds. We use marketing techniques like 3D mail, which was a "game changer" as Todd Walters would say.

Let me explain 3D mail. First, you must understand that when the seller's home doesn't sell, they get bombarded with mail, phone calls and even people knocking on their door. From all this competition, we have had to really stand out with both superior marketing and in just getting our mail read. Ask yourself where do you sort your mail? Above the trash, right? Well, so does your prospect.

So one of the mailings to an expired listing is inside an actual bank bag. You know the green bank bags you would carry a deposit to the bank in? Inside the bank bag is a message that connects the dots like: "After you hire me you're going to need this bag to bring all the money you make to the bank". This was a great tool to get the potential customer to notice us and call us. I can track over $500,000 of commission earned by this one idea.

All of this marketing knowledge led me to test radio with a lot of confidence. Our message was the same that was working in direct mail and other print media. The only difference was that we put a twist on radio by having local celebrities endorse our message. This is called celebrity endorsement and this has opened up the lead funnel even further.

We are now on three radio stations generating hundreds of buyer and seller leads. Once they reach us, we use our systematic approaches to convert them and build loyalty.

To better explain how we do this, let me share with you this flow chart I got from the Craig Proctor Coaching Program.

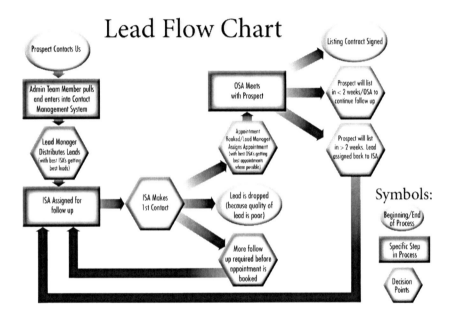

Lead Flow Chart

This chart details how we handle the leads. ISA means Inside Sales Agent. I learned from Craig that it's better to give leads to an Inside Sales Agent and give appointments to Outside Sales Agents. This way we are more productive, with everyone doing only the things they are really good at and enjoy.

We met a great teacher and put into action what he taught. Craig's teaching was able to change our paradigm from working in our business to working on our business. What I mean by that is that most people are running around to meet inspectors, doing a CMA, taking photos or banging signs in the ground. That's working in your business. The problem with that is many of those jobs are $10 an hour jobs. Meanwhile, the jobs that will increase revenue into your business are not being completed, like creating new marketing campaigns, creating new business, training your team or building your team. Working on the business will build your business and create better service for your client. Working in your business will make it so you are always working and will be until the day you quit the business or die behind a desk. I love marketing and working on improving systems to give better service and results to our clients. The more time I spend on that, the better my business is for those that matter most; my clients.

Nathan Clark

While Nathan's success in real estate has deservedly earned him worldwide attention, what's even more impressive than the number of homes he's sold is the speed with which he attained this success. At the age of 20, Nathan was making $14,000 a year sweeping floors on a cruise ship with absolutely no real estate or business background.

A year later, he'd closed 27 residential transactions, and four years after that – still under the age of 30 – he topped the RE/MAX charts in commissions earned by closing more than 130 properties. He was the youngest team leader ever to be number one for the company in RI. Nathan was also the youngest to receive the Hall of Fame Award in 2011 in RI which is awarded to those who have attained over $1 million or more in commissions. He then went on to become the #1 Team in the state of RI amongst all real estate companies in the state of RI by 29 years old.

But Clark's numbers have only careened upward. In 2012, Clark sold 198 homes, making him #1 Team statewide again for the 2 years in a row. Clark has consistently helped 1,000s of homes sell per year for over 12 years now (Nathan sells a home every 24 hours) locally; he has shattered all state sales records. Operating throughout Rhode Island Southern Massachusetts and Eastern Connecticut. Clark has held the distinction of being the top team out of all teams in the entire state for several years.

So how did this young man go from a deck hand to internationally recognized super-salesman in less than a decade? Clark credits his phenomenal success to the innovative and aggressive ways he has approached his real estate business from Craig Proctor. Without previous real estate experience, he entered the business with no preconceived notions of how things should be done, or how high "up" could be. With a tendency for funnel vision, rather than tunnel vision, he not only studied the real estate industry, but also businesses outside the industry to understand what made them successful and how their success could be translated to real estate when he met Craig Proctor. Craig Proctor, the creator of The Quantum Leap Real Estate Success System, which innovatively applies the concepts of leverage, specialization and systemization to provide superior real estate service for his customers, and a superior quality of life for himself and his family. Clark was schooled in the discipline of marketing by Craig Proctor, and marketing has become his passion. He has learned through firsthand experience how to use marketing to get prospective buyers and sellers knocking on his door. Clark has become engaged with thousands of fellow agents across Canada and the U.S. through Mr. Proctor as he openly shares his step-by-step approach to success.

He is an anticipated speaker at company sales rallies, international conventions and seminars, allowing him to share his winning strategies and techniques in a series of products, seminars and coaching programs and has been awarded several prestigious marketing awards in this program.

For More Information Contact Nathan Clark at 401-232-7661

Chapter 16
Leads, Leads, Leads

by Laura Petersen & Todd Walters

To Grow Your Business You Must Have an Overflow of it

The primary reason most agents can't grow their business beyond themselves is that they lack the business to do it. They get some referrals, they buy a few leads from some internet system, have a few past clients coming back and that is just enough business to keep them busy, even comfortable. But enough business to grow their job into a real working business, a highly profitable sales team? No way.

There were plenty of months in my own business over the course of 20+ years of selling a lot of houses where we would generate well over 1,000 leads. My business grew every year I was selling real estate, right up to when I retired from selling homes and took up Coaching. Yes, there were plenty of leads to go around, what I called OVERFLOW, and this created the opportunity for growth.

It does not matter whether you are selling 50 homes, or 500 homes, if you do not have overflow, you do not have opportunity for growth. But what kind of overflow?

It's no secret that YOU are probably not interested in working with buyers or sellers that YOU are not in alignment with. You do have a specific kind of client you most like, bypassing others to get to those. There is nothing wrong with that. This is a SERVICE related business; people sell homes, not machines or ads. So better for all to end up with those who they align with.

So just how do you attract an overflow of the kinds of buyers and sellers that you must want? Craig and I believe that we are experts at this. We are well beyond proving that. In fact, as you read this book you will discover that just about all of the contributing authors are experts at it as well.

*Laura Peterson, a Platinum and Titanium Level Member from Celebration, FL, is excellent at not just generating leads, but at getting the kinds of leads she most likes. You can learn a lot from studying how Laura does things. As you will discover when reading her words on the subject, she is a BIG fan of what we teach, but make no mistake about it, she has to be good at lead generation. Her primary market is not a buyer's primary home; it's their second, or vacation home. – **Todd Walters***

Happy leads, happy agent, happy clients

by Laura Petersen

The first step to mastering the Craig Proctor system and my business was to generate a steady stream of buyers and sellers. The cornerstone to every business is its customer base. And through following the lead of Craig Proctor and Todd Walters, I am able to generate as many leads as the brokerage needs and the type of leads that I want to target.

In conjunction with finding the leads, another aspect of the Craig Proctor system teaches you to analyze the market. This allows you to evaluate where the market is heading and not only be prepared as the market is changing, but be proactive so you don't suffer as many ups and downs in your business. I now target clients that are fun to work with, and consequently, bring the most profit. It is great to be able to be proactive about your business, instead of reactive. Since I started with the Craig Proctor Coaching Program, the Orlando market has been a roller coaster ride . . . in 2007, the market was tanking. Homes had been sitting on the market for long periods of time, and in addition to the values plummeting, the number of properties selling in the marketplace decreased by over 50%. Inventory was at an all-time high. So I was looking for BUYERS . . . and through Craig's system, I found a lot of buyers.

After a time, I could see that the market was changing again, the number of sales was increasing . . . so you would think you would want sellers . . . but in analyzing everything, short sales and bank-owned properties were crowding 70% of the market and did so for over 3 years. I knew that this meant that I should stick with the buyers, and the good news is that the ones we targeted were cash buyers, who we were able to find easily by running the advertising from Craig's system. We also had the ability to work with corporate accounts, which we did on a limited basis. At the time, seller and corporate demands were out of control and there was downward pressure on the commission side from sellers . . . so we were able to confirm that buyers were the way to go.

A couple of years ago, the percentage of distressed properties was finally decreasing, with over 90% of the sales being below $300,000, which were our target buyers and sellers. We weren't content to stop there though; we also targeted the higher end of the market that was selling. One thing that I learned that has always stuck with me is that I can't control the market; I can only control what I do with the market. I am constantly looking for the best strategy. And the best strategy is to always offer what the marketplace wants, whether I personally have it or not.

To find out what the marketplace truly wants at any one given time is really quite simple. I look at MLS, see what kinds of homes are selling like hotcakes, and if I don't have any listings like that, I simply do a search to find other agents' listings that match these criteria. I create ads for lists of properties and pepper those ads everywhere that buyers go to look for real estate in my marketplace. Those prospects that respond are sent the lists that I have pulled from MLS.

I have learned that most agents offer what they have, and for most, that is either their listings, that are not selling, OR themselves. I think this is why so many agents fail. Marketing 101 is to figure out what buyers want, specifically what kinds of houses, where, how much, features and benefits those homes have to offer, and create ads that offer that. It really is that simple.

Using statistics to find who we need to target is one piece of the puzzle. But that is not the only piece to the puzzle. With the coaching of Craig Proctor and Todd Walters, there are a lot of choices as to what ads we wanted to run, what type we would run, and where we would run them. To a certain extent it was an educated guess, but not entirely. Another component of the system was, and still is, testing the ads and constantly knowing their effectiveness.

After I had done much testing to find the perfect formula to bring me the buyers I wanted, I was able to develop the perfect ad that would provide me 100's of leads each month. But here's the interesting thing, as the market changed, the effectiveness of that ad changed as well. Because of Craig's system, we are able to track where every buyer or seller lead comes from, and as the effectiveness changes, we are on top of it and know immediately what to change and how to test to find the next winner. This has been especially helpful as technology has changed. Some media, like newspapers that you may have guessed would be outdated, can still be the best source of people that you want to work with. Some internet advertising is good, some great, and some a dog with fleas, but you don't know until you test it.

Another ingredient to finding the right clients to work with is the message-to-market match. As I earlier stated, there are times when one type of ad works great and then when the market changes it loses its effectiveness. So again, testing the best message for the best results in order to reach the customer that you are looking for is the key. Through coaching with Craig and Todd, I have found that having the masters look at what I'm ready to test has a huge impact on the ad's success. There may be one word or one phrase that provides a better result and that maximizes both the quality and the quantity of those that respond.

In fact, we actually have a word list that we pick from when writing ads. You can take a look at part of the word list here.

Hot Words
for Classified Ads

	FIRST TIME BUYERS (Hot Buttons: SAFETY, Comfort, Protection & Security)	TRADE- UP BUYERS (Hot Buttons: ESTEEM, Prestige & Status)
Words to describe the area or neighborhood	• Wonderful area • Safe neighborhood • Quiet Street • Great Area	• Prestigious address • Exclusive area • Upscale area • Gated community • Executive area
Words to describe the house in general	• Family home • Lovely • Comfortable • Clean • Beautiful	• Elegant • Luxury • Cultured • Grand • Stunning
Words to describe the exterior of the house (the property)	• Trees • Shaded backyard • Patio • Deck • Private yard (patio, deck, etc.) • Big yard (large deck etc.) • Sliding glass doors to deck • Privacy fenced backyard	• Trees • Shade • Private • Professionally landscaped • Wooded backyard • Huge private yard • Golf Course location
Words to describe the inside of the house	• Fireplace • 2 baths (NEVER 1 1/2 baths) • 3 bedroom (NEVER 2 bed rooms; instead of 4 bed rooms say 3 bedrooms + office, 4th bedroom) • Family room • Cozy den • All new (or brand new) kitchen (or bathroom) • Garage (if you live in a snowbelt)	• French doors • Cathedral ceiling • Stunning decor • impressive • Perfect for entertaining • Gourmet kitchen • Magnificent decor • Gorgeous view • Open concept

Together, all of these foundational items add to finding great leads in all stages of the business, and sets the stage for a quantum leap in business!

Chapter 17
Why Follow Up is Everything

by Warren Flax and Craig Proctor

Over the course of this book, you've been given the basic framework to build your ARPS (Automatic Reverse Prospecting System):

- I've explained how to fill your pipeline with ready-to-act prospects by running direct response ads (a combination of classified, editorial-style and USP ads (Step 1)
- I then detailed how you easily sort and sift the leads from your ads into degrees of prospect-readiness by directing the leads to your website where it does the work for you (Step 2)

So now, we'll talk about your Follow-Up System (Step 3).

One of my coaches, Warren Flax from Philadelphia, is excellent at converting leads to appointments. After I lay out the framework of my follow up system here, I hand things off to Warren who has written a few words about this from his perspective (see below).

Follow up is an EXTREMELY critical step to get right. If you don't get Step 3 right, you will have basically wasted all the time and money you invested in Steps 1-2.

You see, Steps 1-2 (Automatic Reverse Prospecting System) will have provided you with some excellent leads - prospects who have raised their hands and told you that they were moving. If you fail to follow-up promptly, professionally, and systematically with these people, YOU WILL LOSE THEM.

I know this with certainty because it happened to me. In fact, you wouldn't believe the wastage that occurs in our industry. I'll illustrate this important point by telling you about my own personal experience.

Several years ago, when I was still trying to put all the pieces of the puzzle in place, I did an analysis on my business which shocked and depressed me. Let me explain. At this point in time, I had the automatic reverse prospecting part of my business working well. In fact, I had hundreds of leads coming into my business, and all these leads were dutifully entered into my contact management system.

HOWEVER, because I hadn't firmly put a foolproof system in place to ensure that these leads were followed up properly, I knew I wasn't converting as many of these prospects as I could. The question was, how bad was it? I decided to find out.

I was devastated by the results . . .

I cross-matched my database of seller prospects (which I had generated through my ARPS) against all new listings (by all agents) on MLS. Astonishingly, I found that 82% of my seller prospects listed within 12 months. Now understand, these were prospects who had contacted me FIRST (i.e. they were prospects who had requested one of my reports, or who had attended one of my Tours etc.) In other words, these were people who had TOLD me they were thinking of moving. They'd raised their hands and qualified themselves.

That part was good. After all, it helped me validate that the quality of leads I was generating with my ARPS was high. HOWEVER, because my follow-up system was not yet fully up to speed, I only converted 17% of this 82%. In other words, I LOST the balance of these prospects to other agents!

That was a turning point for me. That was the point when it became crystal clear to me that simply finding a better way to generate the lead was far from enough. In fact, by becoming so good at generating leads, I had inadvertently created another problem: i.e. too many leads to follow-up on (unless I found a way to automate this process).

And this is where Step 3 comes in. Step 3 is a Follow-Up system which can significantly improve the conversion of your prospect database into face-to-face appointments. I swore I would NEVER allow the waste and lost opportunity described above to happen again. As a result, the Follow-Up System I teach agents now incorporates a much finer "sifting" element which not only does a better job of grading the quality and urgency of the leads, but also gives you the opportunity to respond appropriately, and with due urgency to these prospects.

You see, a mistake I was making before was lumping all FUTURE prospects together. Let me explain. When I graded a lead, I'd put it into one of three categories: NOW business, FUTURE business, and DUD leads. I'd delete the DUD leads, attempt to convert the NOW business to appointments immediately, and then put all the FUTURE business onto the same basic follow up plan. Even though some of these future prospects were less qualified and some were "golden prospects", great prospects that had clearly indicated to me that they were definitely going to list their home for sale (i.e. maybe they had already bought a new home, or were being transferred, etc.) I knew that it was a matter of when not if with these prospects. So as you can see, the mistake I was making was treating the Golden Prospects and the Less Qualified Prospects in the exact same manner -- even knowing this important difference, both the golden and the lukewarm prospects would get the same follow-up calls and written follow-up. The only difference between the way I treated the two was the scheduled frequency of the calls. And you saw the results of that. Doing things the old way, I only managed to convert about 17% of these FUTURE seller prospects -- not quite 1 in 5.

What I started to realize is that I needed a way to respond more aggressively to what prospects were telling me in terms of timing so I didn't miss them just because I happened to be a week out in my phone call.

I needed to find a way to have my website and hotline separate my leads into "hot prospects" and "warm prospects" so that I could prioritize my call backs. After giving this much thought, I arrived at a solution. I would have my prospects themselves tell me if they were "hot" or "warm".

I did this by adding a simple prompt on both my website and my hotline. On each landing page on my website the prospect is provided a form to fill out with their personal information, such as name, address, phone number and email address - along with the type of information they are requesting. There is also a small box on this form where they are asked to check if they want to receive "Report #1" or "Report #2". It is explained that Report #1 is for those who are thinking of making a move in the next 6 months or less, and that Report #2 is for those who are thinking of moving in longer than 6 months. Of course, on my hotline, this same prompt is included at the end of the script.

Let me take a step back and describe the base follow-up system. It's important to do this first, because the base system underlies everything. All FUTURE leads (golden or lukewarm) still receive this basic follow up. The more advanced follow up plan for golden leads is in addition to this base plan. So let's explore the base plan now.

My 4 Step Follow-Up System

Obviously, all your leads need to be followed up no matter where they come from. When you meet a prospect at your Tour of Homes, or if a prospect calls your office directly off a sign or property display ad, you'll need to schedule regular follow-up with them in order to convert this lead into a face-to-face appointment.

For the leads generated through your ARPS, however, there are some specific additional steps you must take in order to convert this caller (who, you remember, contacted you because you gave them an easy and non-threatening way to get the information they were after WITHOUT having to speak with an agent) into a prospect who will be receptive to speaking with you about their relocation plans on a regular basis (i.e. someone who you can schedule into your contact management system for follow-up calls and written communication). Depending on how ready-to-act the prospect is, the length of time and the number of calls or letters may vary, but the essence and order of the steps is the same no matter whether the prospect is requesting a free special report, a hotlist, or a property listing printout.

Thus, Step 3 for leads generated by my website and hotline is four mini-steps which commence once the prospect leaves their contact information. The 4 steps are as follows:

1. **Access the names, addresses and phone numbers of prospects who have left you their contact information** in order to receive the information offered in your ad (e.g. free special report, property information etc.) and note which report they asked for (i.e. #1 or #2). Your website and Hotline leads should go directly to your smart phone.

2. **Because most prospects will leave you their email address, you will email the following information:**

    - A cover letter that references the attached list of homes or special report, and also promotes you and offers further reports/services

- Send the information as soon as possible - IMPORTANT NOTE: Never, Never, Never switch the auto responder on your website to "on". If your prospects receive the requested information instantaneously, through the auto responder, what reason do you have to contact them in your follow up call? Remember, your follow up call always starts with, "The reason I'm calling is to let you know that we received your request for "(the information)" and we've sent that to you." Using the auto responder eliminates the very reason that you give the prospect for your contacting him or her.

If the prospect does not leave you their email address, the report must be sent:

- In a hand-addressed plain envelope with live postage
- With a cover letter
- As soon as possible

NOTE: If a prospect asks for both reports 1 and 2 (which sometimes happens), you can enclose another related report.

3. Enter the names, addresses and telephone numbers of each prospect into your contact management system, as well as which report they requested (i.e. Report #1 or Report #2).

NOTE: These first 3 steps are completed by an assistant, not by you. I'm sure you'll agree that anyone could complete these tasks. It would not be a good use of your time. You will get involved only at the next point to make the follow-up call to those who requested Report #1 (i.e. the prospects who represent NOW business). In my own business, and in the businesses of my successful members, those prospects who requested Report #2 are handed over to your Inside Sales Agent (ISA) as they will require more long-term follow-up until they are ready-to- act. If you do not yet have an Inside Sales Agent, the sifting and sorting information (that Report #1/#2 provide you) is still extremely useful.

Remember, your new problem is HAVING TOO MANY LEADS TO FOLLOW UP WITH IN A TIMELY MANNER. The automatic sifting and sorting gives you an objective way of prioritizing these leads. If you simply don't have time to call all of them back within the prescribed time (asap), at least make sure you call all the Report #1's by then. This isn't a perfect situation as you really should be following up all leads as soon as possible, but this will at least increase your NOW business, which should increase your cash flow and make it possible for you to eventually hire an assistant.

4. Call the prospects who requested information and use the Universal Call Back Script (available to Quantum Leap members). The purpose of this call is to:

    a. Establish top-of-mind consciousness with these prospects in a nonthreatening manner
    b. Probe them with qualifying questions to help you understand the quality and time frame of the lead
    c. Schedule an appointment if they do represent an immediate opportunity
    d. Put them on the right Follow-Up Plan (including both written and verbal follow-up) if they are a longer term opportunity.

What you do with these prospects after this point will depend on how your call goes. Here's what I teach agents to do:

- **NOW BUSINESS** - set up a meeting to present your listing/buyer presentation to them

- **FUTURE BUSINESS – For Seller Prospects** - I divide the category of FUTURE business into three segments:

  - those who indicate they will definitely list within 3 months or less and are open to using me (these prospects are put onto what I call my Gold Plan #1)
  - those who indicate they will definitely list within 6 months and are open to using me (these prospects are put onto my Gold Plan #2)
  - those who indicate they plan to move in greater than 6 months - schedule follow-up on my contact management system and send them my Market Watch monthly newsletter

- **FUTURE BUSINESS - For Buyer Prospects:** They are really only placed into one segment that captures all buyers who are not "Now Business":

- They receive my monthly Market Watch newsletter and my regularly scheduled follow up calls

- **DUD LEAD** - delete them from the system if they are working with another agent or if they have indicated clearly that they're not moving (or are just plain rude.)

Relationship-Building is Important

It is critical to note that communicating with a prospect (or a client for that matter) is not a one-shot deal. People are inundated with information - you may have to communicate with them two, ten, twenty times before they respond. Be careful to do this respectfully so you don't become a nuisance, but never forget that . . .

> **. . . if you don't have top-of-mind consciousness, your prospects will forget all about you**

More to the point, as I found out from first-hand experience, they'll find someone else who is paying attention (or who just happens to be in the right place at the right time, where you were in the right place at the wrong time) - like your competitor.

I carefully schedule follow-up calls using my contact management system which systemizes my prospect communications so prospects don't fall through the cracks.

Many of the prospects generated by your ARPS will represent FUTURE business. This will be particularly true of the leads generated by your editorial-style ads where roughly 80% of calls will be from prospects who are not ready-to-act immediately, but who are thinking of making a move in the next 12 months.

You may ask why you should be bothered working with these longer-term prospects. Why not simply run classified ads which generate more NOW business. Well, the fact is, the closer prospects are to making a move, the greater the likelihood that they've aligned themselves with another agent. If you catch them early in the process, before they've had the time to form such alliances, you stand a greater chance of converting them into your client.

Besides, if you systemize your follow up with this future business, there will come a point in time (if you've followed up consistently) when this future business will convert to now business. Every week you'll have leads that you cultivated months ago suddenly turn current. Why wouldn't you want to easily double, triple or more the number of prospects who want to act NOW and are predisposed to working with you?

That's pretty obvious isn't it? But it's an important point to reinforce, particularly if you have a Team, who may not have the foresight to be patient. I know my Team did a lot of complaining at first about some of the leads that were given to them. If the lead didn't convert into business within the next two weeks, they whined about it being a poor lead. Well, it's not a poor lead, it's simply a future prospect, and with the right follow-up, as mentioned, future will become now.

One of the tools I use to stay in touch with this future group is my Market Watch newsletter. Published every month, this newsletter discusses issues that have top-of-mind relevance for those thinking of making a move.

Let's hear, now, from Warren Flax on this important topic . . .

✦ ✦ ✦

Nothing Replaces Calling Back The Leads. Nothing!

by Warren Flax

How distressing it must be for some home sellers to find out that their real estate agent, the person they have hired to get a buyer for their home, doesn't return buyer calls for 24-to-48 hours, if ever. Leaves 1 or 2 messages for an interested buyer and then gives up. Assumes that it's the prospect's job to call them back. Has no system for tracking and following up with down-the-road buyer prospects. Doesn't know what to say to compel a motivated buyer to want to meet with them.

Now imagine hiring an agent who is so good at follow-up that hundreds of real estate agents pay for the privilege of learning what he has to say on the phone? How he structures his database to ensure maximum efficiency? Whose systems are so effective that he can run a real estate team at peak efficiency where buyer prospects become face-to-face meetings; who then become signed buyer clients who are predisposed to buying his sellers' homes?

Well, that describes me and how my business works in Pennsylvania and New Jersey. At any given time I have between 625 and 1,000 buyers in my database, actively seeking homes in Bucks, Mercer and Burlington counties. Trained by world renowned real estate trainer Craig Proctor, I have built an entire company serving the Philadelphia metro region on the concept of efficient follow-up. Phone calls are returned. Internet requests are pounced upon. Emails are responded to by multiple parties. Homes are sold. Lots of them. In 2014, I was named by RealTrends and The Wall Street Journal as one of the top 250 real estate agents in the United States (there are more than 1,000,000 licensees.)

The sad truth of most salespeople is that they simply don't follow up. National studies indicate that

- 48% of sales people <u>never</u> follow up with a prospect
- 25% of sales people make a second contact and stop
- 12% of sales people make more than three contacts

Just as the overwhelming majority of salespeople are giving up, the Buyers are starting to get ready to take action. From the same national studies:

- 2% of sales are made on the first contact
- 3% of sales are made on the second contact
- 5% of sales are made on the third contact
- 10% of sales are made on the fourth contact
- 80% of sales are made on the fifth to twelfth contact

So if a real estate broker doesn't have a system for maintaining contact and follow-up with each and every prospect over a period of months and even years, the broker is likely to be inefficient and unable to run a profitable business getting their clients' homes sold.

System & Technology

My Team follows the Craig Proctor system exclusively. Every prospect is quickly entered into a live, cloud-based database while simultaneously alerting multiple team members. Inside Sales agents respond to phone, internet and email inquiries and book appointments with licensed agents to meet with and cultivate ready-to-act, as well as down-the-road prospects.

Script

Using Craig Proctor's time-tested Universal Follow-up script, my team is able to quickly and courteously determine each prospect's individual timing and motivation. By following a simple script, the caller offers each prospect the most appropriate options for their particular situation – maybe a free monthly newsletter to keep them up to date with market trends, or maybe a face-to-face meeting with a skilled agent to help them begin their home search.

Training

Daily, weekly and monthly training are the keys to my team's efficiency. Utilizing video conferencing, conference calling and live team training allows each team member the attention they need to ensure they are peak efficient with conversion.

All of these systems, technology, scripting and training blends together to create a seamless process for home buyers to buy my listings. The end result is that according to TREND MLS statistics, my seller clients average 3.8% higher sold prices than the area average, in less time and with less hassle.

Warren Flax

A 2002 MBA/MA Graduate from the Wharton School and the Joseph A Lauder Institute of the University of Pennsylvania, Warren Flax was initially licensed in real estate in 2003 and founded Platinum Realty Team in 2008, with licenses in Pennsylvania and New Jersey. In 2013 Warren was named by RealTrends/Wall Street Journal as one of the top 250 real estate agents in the United States (out of more than 1,000,000). A former network television sportscaster, Warren has appeared and been promoted on NBC, CBS, ABC, ESPN Radio and WPST locally. He regularly speaks before real estate audiences on the topic of lead conversion and database management. He has authored numerous articles on the subject and can be contacted at 215-945-3000 in Pennsylvania or 609-301-5622 in New Jersey or online at www.WarrenFlax.com

Chapter 18
Price is Elastic

by Carol Royse

Increasing the Amount of Money You Make Per Transaction

"Cost is only a factor in the absence of value" - ***Todd Walters***

I have learned there are 3 ways to grow my real estate business:

1. Increase the number of transactions.
2. Increase the amount of money made per transaction.
3. Increase the number of times a client comes back and buys from our Team

There seems to be regular discussion and training about getting more closings and getting clients to come back and buy. BUT . . . there seems to be little discussion about increasing the amount of money you make per transaction.

In fact in all of my 20+ years of selling real estate, the ONLY place I have heard or been trained on increasing the amount of money I make per transaction is from Craig Proctor Coaching.

Many agents say that their expenses are up, income is down, and think the solution is to simply sell a higher priced home. But that's no guarantee of increased income per transaction. It's quite possible that the higher priced homes are not selling. Moreover, many agents are squeamish about discussion of fees, especially raising them. But what I have discovered is that my clients want better service and results, more value, not less and if the value is there, they will pay for it and give me raving reviews for over delivering.

Price is elastic. As the team leader, it is my job to stretch it. The market will determine what it is willing to pay and accept, based on the value I deliver.

How to increase your income without increasing your number of sales or hours of work is a dilemma many Realtors face. Realtors are working 40, 50, even 60 hours a week, doing all they can to list and close sales of properties. They just can't imagine how they can increase their income. There are only so many hours in day.

I faced this dilemma as well and believed the answer was to increase my cost of sale by bringing additional agents onto my team. While that can help, it is not the entire solution. Even hiring administrative staff support is a help. There is payroll to cover plus you have become a "manager" of people. You may have more time, but there is an additional cost of doing business. That cost is less GCI for you, and in many cases, more "brain drain" in management and employee problems or challenges.

After years of running in circles in this scenario, I finally found the solution for me and my team. First, by implementing the systems I learned from Craig Proctor, buyers and sellers began to see the difference I brought to the sale of their home. Getting the seller top dollar in the least amount of time with the least amount of hassle to them is not just a catchy phrase. When I applied proven systems, sellers became more than willing to pay a premium to get their property sold.

As for a buyer, when they were convinced our team could find them the best home at the best price, they had no problem with paying a fee **beyond** what was being offered in the MLS to the buyer agent. It all comes down to the value offered to the client or customer.

Quite simply, to increase your GCI income, raise your fee

(commission)! Not only did I raise my commission to the seller by a full percent, but I lowered the commission offered to the buyer agent in the MLS. For example, when taking a listing consider raising your fee by 0.5% to 1.0%. You could also consider offering 1.0% to 0.5% less to the buyer agent. We will use an average sales price of $300,000. Prior to realizing how much more I brought to the table in knowledge and premiere enhanced systems to the seller, my fee would be a full percent less than that of the buyer's agent to entice them to show my listing. That was faulty thinking!

So, let's look at the numbers again. $300,000 sales price with an additional 1.0% equals $3,000. And the 0.5% reduction to the buyer agent equals $1,500. This is money that can be used for enhanced marketing and administrative help or other expenses. I have not found the buyer agent who would not show and write an offer on a home because of a reduced fee!

On the buyer side, in our Buyer Loyalty Agreement, we collect a higher fee than is normally offered in the MLS. When we explain to the buyer we will buy back their home if they are not satisfied with it, and additionally we will ask the seller to pay the difference between the commission deficiency and our fee, buyers have no problem in agreeing to the terms in the loyalty agreement.

Of course, there are other ways to increase your GCI by not increasing your work load or hours. Increase your average sales price. Work two areas, one a first time home buyer neighborhood and another move up buyer. Move up to the higher end properties but have a very visible presence in the area of move up buyers who would be interested in the higher end properties. Here's how I made this work; I have homes listed in a $500,000 neighborhood area where many home buyers are looking for properties in the $800,000 to $1,000,000 price range. I list the $500,000 they are selling and sell them the $1,000,000 home! Imagine those numbers at the higher fee.

Throughout all of these adjustments to my business, you will notice I did not say I worked longer hours, or had to sell more homes to increase my Gross Commission Income. My goal, and hopefully your goal as an agent, is to have a quality life, time to spend with family and friends; living the lifestyle you desire. It is possible, with comprehensive systems and expert coaching. Have the courage to try what others say is impossible, and you can achieve your goals.

Now with more time, you are ready to expand to buyer agents and listing agents. Duplicate yourself by teaching them these same principals. They will stay with you on your team because not only are they making more money, but having a quality of life experience. It's all in the training and systems where you offer superior service and deliver an outstanding result to home sellers and home buyers.

Any new program or idea can be daunting. It takes the mindset of a business owner and the training and accountability of Team Members to carry out the new procedures. I have found that being a leader and showing the way by example, my Team will follow.

✦ ✦ ✦

Carol Royse, CEO; Carol Royse Team

Carol Royse is a Real Estate Icon in the Metro Phoenix area, having been licensed for over 33 years. Joined by her Daughter, Vikki Royse Middlebrook, and her son, Timothy Evans, the Carol Royse Team is nationally and regionally recognized as a top Team in Arizona. The Team has been featured in many real estate journals and publications including the Wall Street Journal, television and radio. Royse and the Team serve home sellers, home buyers as well as many investor clients in the US and Internationally.

A strong advocate of business coaching, Carol, Vikki and Tim have been members of Craig Proctor Coaching since 2000 and have recently joined the prestigious Titanium Coaching Program with Coach and Trainer, Todd Walters. No one succeeds alone is not a cliché with Royse and the Team, but it is lived out each day. Supporting the team is a 2 person marketing department and 3 full time licensed Administrative Assistants as well as 6 Listing/Buyer Specialists. Covering the entire Metro Phoenix area as well as the State of Arizona, The Carol Royse Team is highly organized and trained for optimal customer service and results.

Chapter 19
Networking Without Work

by Sam Wilson

You Are a Walking Talking Billboard or At Least Should Be

When used properly, networking can be an engine – one that drives you to success. For me that meant becoming a top producing real estate agent, but the possibilities are endless for professionals in every field when you know how to network, and more importantly, know how to network well. In this chapter we will talk about both, along with developing and nurturing your network once you have one.

First, a bit about me. As I mentioned, I'm in real estate, have a very solid profitable real estate sales team, but it's not where I started out. My career began in sales and marketing with a variety of Fortune 500 companies. There I was essentially given my own clients, working within the framework set up for me by my bosses. It's great when you think about it – someone giving you clients or a network to mine clients from – because it's so much easier to be handed something ready to use than to toil to create something from the ground up. But in 2001 I transitioned to a career in real estate, and suddenly I had to build my own clientele, something I had never done before. When faced with that task, I had to learn pretty quickly how to efficiently find clients.

The key word here is efficient. Whether you are starting out in your own business, new to an established business, or just hoping to reinvigorate your business or career, we all have to work efficiently. What can you do in a short span of time to offer the highest rewards?

There are any number of ways to find new clients – like the tried and true practice of "prospecting" – door knocking, open houses, blind mailing, advertising, sales scripts, and the like. Doesn't sound like fun, does it? In truth, it's not. It's a lot of door slamming, dealing with people you don't like, and lots and lots of rejection. It's also not very effective – in addition to being time consuming and expensive. The vast majority of strangers you meet will turn you down, or forget as soon as you've left their sight. As any prospector will tell you, prospecting is a numbers game and rarely are the odds ever in your favor.

Networking offers a lot of advantages over those cold calls or mass mailings. First, you get a better quality of clientele – because you choose them. Hopefully, you will choose people who are interested in you, your product or your service, or are likely to be interested in it in the future. Second, you are not a stranger. Networking is about building relationships. When people know you, you are elevated in their eyes beyond the rank of telemarketer, ambulance chaser or tax collector, which will work in your favor when it comes to finding new business. Third, networking allows you to focus on what you do best: your product or service. Instead of "chasing numbers" you are performing your job, which for me meant matching the right person with the right property. Finally, it's also a lot less expensive, because you aren't relying on random advertising or mailing campaigns to find clients.

In short, networking saves you time and money, and offers greater rewards. What's not to like?

If you've gotten this far, you probably have some sort of idea about what networking is. However, for the sake of clarity before we go any further, let's define exactly what we are talking about when we say "network" or "networking." A network is a system or structure with interconnecting bonds. For our purposes, think of it as a system or structure of people, bonded by common experiences, goals, interests, needs or talents. Networking refers to the exchange of information or assistance among those having mutual interests and/or benefits. The key word here is exchange – all successful networking relationships are a two-way street. So be prepared to give, if you expect someday to receive.

Let's take that definition of networking a step further, and call it the active pursuit of meaningful relationships, finding ways to give to those who can help you the most, adding value to other people's lives, learning to ask them to help you, and receiving that help joyfully. If you want to be successful at networking, all of those elements must be part of your strategy.

And having a strategy is absolutely vital when it comes to networking successfully. The more focused you are in your approach, the easier it will be to achieve your ultimate goal: get those who use you to use and refer you more. Of course, you also want those who don't use you to use and refer you as well.

Most networking strategies have three objectives in common. The first objective must be to build lasting relationships of mutual benefit that will produce a recurring source of business for a lifetime. The second objective should be to work, primarily, with people you like. The third should be to build a valuable database that can be sold someday for continuing financial returns.

However, before you can accomplish any of these objectives, you have to know how to network. It's more than just introducing yourself to people, handing them a business card and calling it a day. Meeting people is important, but it's equally important to build trust with them. You want them to remember, to do business with and recommend you. Deepen your relationship with those you want in your network. Prove your value to them. Help them out with their business in some way before you ask for something in return. When you do ask for something, ask respectfully and receive it joyfully.

Where do you go to meet people? It's not like a dating scene, so you want to avoid singles bars and the produce aisle at your local market. Start with groups you are already involved in because here you will find people with whom you share an interest. Chances are they already know you (and hopefully) trust you in some capacity. Another way to meet people would be to join groups with people and businesses you want to target – like your local Chamber of Commerce, Lions Club or Rotary. You might also try social events – like an auction for your local Boys and Girls Club, organizing a fundraiser for a local charity, speaking engagements to share your knowledge or free seminars on a related topic or industry. There are many, many opportunities out there, so feel free to explore what's available or mastermind new opportunities with peers or coworkers. Find what works for you.

I'm a member of the Denver Metro Chamber of Commerce, which is a great place to learn and grow as a business leader. I became involved with the Chamber's Leads Groups, which consist of small groups of business people who meet to discuss leadership, sales, best practices and more. Each group becomes a tight-knit  community that offers endless opportunities for networking, no matter what your field. When I say I got involved, I don't just mean attended some meetings and chatted with people. I was President of one of the groups, Leads Group One – helping to organize and plan events, speakers and functions. Currently I am chair-elect of the entire program. This isn't work that I get paid for, but it is work that I enjoy with people I enjoy being with, and more importantly, it's helped me develop the sort of strong network that has spurred my career in real estate.

Once you find your group or groups and the people you want to network with, what do you do? Well, you have to talk to them. Approaching strangers is never an easy task, and it can often be a little awkward, for everyone. But chances are that if you are part of these groups hoping to network, the person you are hoping to talk to is there for the same reason. So introduce yourself. Ask some questions, like: What do you do for a living? What brought you here? Find some common ground. Eventually, you will have to ask them the big question: If you needed, or knew someone who needed (your product or service), do you have someone you trust to refer them to? (If no, make an appointment.) Also realize that just because someone isn't a potential client today, doesn't mean they won't be one tomorrow.

As I've stated before, meeting people is important, but just meeting them isn't enough. You have to build trust with them. People do business with people they trust. People refer people to people they trust. How do you build trust? It's a two-fold enterprise. **First, you must demonstrate your character. Second, you must demonstrate your competence**. Then, you must do both consistently and repeatedly.

What is character? In this context, it's showing that it's not all about you. Listen to people, especially for their wants and needs. Ask questions about the things that matter – family, occupation, recreation and dreams (or FORD). Remember the special occasions, like birthdays, anniversaries and other milestones. Give unconditionally. Share personal interests. Spend time with people outside of work, and don't talk about work when you do it. These things will show people that you are the sort of person they can trust – and do business with.

While character is an important part of the puzzle, character alone won't help you build a network. Competence is a vital piece, needed to complete the picture. How do you show people you're competent? For starters, do what you say you will do. Be consistent. Be an expert in your field and share your knowledge. Always do more than expected. Show up to everything on time and prepared. Be honest and willing to say "I don't know" when you encounter something you don't know. Be proactive, search for new ideas and be aware of the latest trends and developments in your field. Follow these tips, and your competence will be obvious to all who deal with you.

So, you've met people, collected their contact information, built a relationship with them, and proven yourself competent and trustworthy. Now you have a database. At this point, it's important that you organize that database to see where you stand and where you need to go. Where are the gaps in your network? Who is missing? Once you find those gaps, look for people who might fill them when you attend events. You might even devise a target list of people you want to meet. Always be aware of ways to grow your network, and the direction you want to grow in.

You also want to nurture your network, not just expand it. You do that by staying in touch, and there are many ways to do that – through hand-written note or cards on special occasions, email updates or blog posts about new products or services or a simple phone call to check in with someone to see how they are. Contact is an integral part of maintaining your network. But it has to be contact that is meaningful and valuable to the person you are seeking to maintain contact with. No one wants to open their email to find spam or mailboxes to discover endless clutter. Make it meaningful, make it count.

When it comes time to ask for something – a lead, an introduction or help of any kind – be direct. Ask for what you need and see where it takes you. If you've built a strong network, your success is all but guaranteed.

✦ ✦ ✦

Sam Wilson

Now the Broker/Owner and leader of a highly productive residential real estate firm, Wilson Group Real Estate, Sam has taken his team and his business to the elite level in his marketplace. By offering his clients an unprecedented service commitment known as CLIENTS FIRST, he's been able to provide his clientele with award winning service. The Wilson Group is skilled and experienced in all types of Residential Real Estate. Sam has successfully assisted clients in all neighborhoods of the Denver Metro area and surrounding suburbs. As a result, The Wilson Group has consistently grown volume and transactions each year in a declining market. Previously, Sam was the top agent in an office of 80+ agents. He held this distinction for four years running. Sam and The Wilson Group are consistently one of the top producing agents in the Denver Metro market for Residential Real Estate Agents. In 2002, his first full year of his Real Estate career, Sam was awarded the Rookie of The Year Award at his office and has accelerated and grown every year since then. Sam holds an Employing Broker's level license and has recently been the Employing Broker of his Keller Williams office. He has held several leadership positions in that office including: Training Director; Mentor and Chairman of the Finance Committee for the Agent Leadership Council. Prior to his career in real estate which began in 2001, Sam held several senior sales, marketing and leadership positions at major corporations such as Proctor and Gamble, The Polaroid Corporation and The Coca-Cola Company. He excelled in all positions and was continuously promoted to higher level jobs with more responsibility at each Company.

Sam has always been ranked in the top 1% of all agents and is fast approaching one of the top 10 agents in his marketplace. He is also the proud recipient of the 5280 Five Star Award for customer service every year since 2010. Only 120 out of 22,000 agents in the Denver Market have achieved this prestigious level of the 5280 award.

Sam grew up in Connecticut and Massachusetts, where he attended Northeastern University and graduated with a dual degree in Marketing and Finance in 1985. He is now married and living with his wife Pamela in Golden, Colorado. His hobbies include skiing, cycling, mountain biking, photography, travel, riding motorcycles and driving sports cars. Currently, his 2 favorite business books are *The 21 Irrefutable Laws of Leadership* by John Maxwell and *The E-Myth* by Michael Gerber.

Sam and The Wilson Group are currently affiliated with the National Association of Realtors, the Colorado Association of Realtors, the Denver Metro Association of Realtors. Sam's favorite charity is the National Sports Center For the Disabled (NSCD) to which a portion of the Company income is donated to assist children with disabilities participate in outdoor Colorado sports.

Chapter 20
Leveraging Technology for an Even More Profitable ROI

by Marc Gastineau

Leveraging Leading Edge Technology for an Even More Profitable Real Estate Sales Team

As a real estate professional in the Phoenix Metro area for over 16 years, selling nearly 1,000 homes, and earning millions of dollars in commissions, I want to describe one strategy we have implemented that has automated Craig Proctor's Quantum Leap System in our real estate business.

By utilizing technology we've been able to implement more and more things that we would not have been able to do if we did not have the technology available.

For example, the CP Platinum Coaching program has a superior Expired Listing Marketing Program. It involves a consistent message with a bold USP that is sent to the expired seller and aggressively kept in front of the seller until they choose to meet with you or they relist the home. The process involves a mailing on Day 1, Day 5, Day 10, Day 15, Day 30, Day 90, Day 180 and Day 365. There are also voice blasts that are peppered into the process.

If you had to manage this process on your own using excel spreadsheets or your Outlook calendar, this would quickly become a process that would overwhelm even the smartest marketer. Most agents would stop within a few weeks.

We took the entire CP Platinum Expired Marketing process and built it into our Infusionsoft application. We utilize Virtual Assistants to implement most all the steps required.

A quick example of how this works is the following:

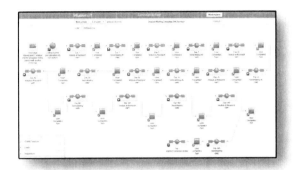

On a daily basis, our Virtual Assistant (VA) pulls the daily expired listings from within our marketplace. This is done utilizing Macros within Firefox so the VA only needs to click a few buttons to get the Excel spreadsheet of that day's expired listings. Then with just one click in Excel all the listings are automatically uploaded into our application via Excel macros.

The moment they are uploaded into our system, the next 12 months of processes are predetermined for this contact (expired listing).

This includes tasks to our VA's in India to check if the property has been relisted, check tax records to find "non-owner" occupants or out of state owners, check if property is an owner agent listing, REO listing or other type of listing we elect to not market to. Once our VA completes the task this automatically triggers a task within our system to our "local" US based VA to hand-address a specific envelope and mail it.

So essentially within 24 hours from the day a listing expires, the processes go back and forth across the globe. On the same day a hand-addressed envelope is mailed and post marked to arrive at the prospect's home the next day. This happens hundreds of times per week in our business, and for a fraction of what we used to pay for an "in office" employee to do the work.

And the best thing is all of this is done without my involvement as the team leader. I just review the reports and oversee the success of our campaigns.

How do you automate your real estate business?

I get asked often, "How do I automate my real estate business"? My answer is "One process at a time". Be careful not to bite off more that you can effectively get done within a few weeks period of time. If you try and change too much at one time you inevitably will end up with a bunch of unfinished projects.

The question a real estate agent needs to ask every day is, "What am I doing today that should or could be automated?"

What are those mundane tasks that you as a team leader or even the agents on your team should not be doing? Everyone has them. We get into this mindset that, "I am the only one that can do this right!" But those thoughts are killers when it comes to automating your business.

Remember automation may start by having your assistant do the tasks you should not be doing. It is better to start small then work into systemizing the entire process.

Another way to look at automating is if you find yourself doing a task 2 to 3 times per day then it is most likely something that should be automated, either by your assistant or some sort of technology.

I have gotten to a point in my real estate business where, frankly, I am unwilling to start any "new" program that cannot be automated.

Make a decision today to find one part of your business that can be systemized, then go to work on getting it done. Don't give up until it is working as you want. Be patient and stick with it. It will be worth it!

Marc Gastineau

Marc Gastineau started his Real Estate Career in 1998 and soon became one of the top real estate salesmen in Phoenix, selling over 100 homes per year. Shortly after beginning his career, he stumbled upon the teaching and systems of Craig Proctor. Using the Quantum Leap System, Marc has been able to sell over 1,000 homes and has one of the top sales teams in Arizona. He has won numerous awards including being listed in the top 10 real estate teams per the Phoenix Business Journal. Marc is also a recipient of the Quantum Leap Award. He prides himself on effectively using the system and training others to become highly successful with it as well. Marc has trained hundreds of agents and continues to coach many other real estate professionals to become the top in their market place.

Marc Gastineau
GASTINEAU REAL ESTATE TEAM
Realty ONE Group
480-661-7700 Ext. 17

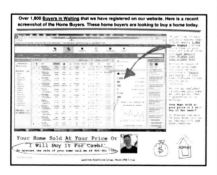

Chapter 21
The Leadership Factor

by François Mackay

Leadership is Required

Taking your real estate business from where it is right now to a Highly Profitable Real Estate Sales Team, going from being the technician in your enterprise to being the strategist, will necessitate a huge dose of leadership.

People sell homes, not ads, not machines, not the internet - people. Skilled people. In order to elevate your business to the next level, the main thing you will need is human resources. And in order to attract, train, motivate and keep your team for a long period of time, you will need to demonstrate leadership.

My coaches, Craig Proctor and Todd Walters, had key people on their team for many, many years; 10, 15, even 20 years. I have discovered that this is a commonality among the most successful agents in North America. They all seem to have key people that have been with them for long periods of time. Bottom line, the most successful agents are good leaders.

I started my career back in 1997, at the age of 21. I joined my mother, who was already a very successful real estate agent and one of the very first agents in Quebec to hire an assistant. She taught me how to be a great real estate agent and showed me how to manage my first assistant. Five years later, she retired and I carried on with one assistant to build my real estate Team. I now have 30 agents and 10 administrative assistants and am always growing.

In this chapter I will share my knowledge and advice on how to build a great team, and just as important, how to lead that team.

Leadership means you have to connect to other people in such a way that they want to follow you, do things for you, be a part of something YOU believe in. You have to convince them that what you are presently doing is incredible and that what you want to accomplish is exceptional. You want them to feel that they are part of the big picture.

There are different types of real estate team leaders, but in today's world the dictator is not appreciated. The perfect leader in today's real estate market has to involve people in what he or she believes, by giving them the opportunity to speak, to be heard, to feel important. He or she has to show them how it's done and give them the right tools to achieve their goals. The team leader needs to connect to other people in a way that conveys how much they are appreciated and must also reward their efforts when they produce good work.

Let's look at 3 different scenarios where your leadership will be needed in building your team.

If you are a solo agent and want to start growing your team, you will first need to hire an administrative person. I went through many assistants when I first started to build my team. Some of them were there for the job only, they needed money and they did an alright job, but not more than what I asked. You can really tell when someone loves their job. They will stay after hours when needed and they will care about your customers as much as you do. As my coach, Todd Walters says, "the idea is to take it slow at first when hiring, but be quick to fire". I also recommend that you use the DISC personality test to hire. It will help you identify the right candidate for the right job. But in the long run, this employee will

have to be led by you if you want to get the maximum productivity out of them.

To express your leadership and gain your first follower, you will need to define the BIG WHY ! Like Simon Sinek mentioned in his talk, "How great leaders inspire action", you have to define the reason you are in business, why is it important that you do what you do, and mostly, why your assistants must care about what you do. If you inspire your employees and they believe in your cause, this will propel your business to another level. Only then have you truly duplicated yourself through your team.

Before I got into real estate, I worked at the McDonald's that my father-in-law owned. I really appreciated the structure of the company. I got to move up in the company by first becoming a trainer, then a team leader and finally, a manager. It was not because of my contact, it was actually quite the opposite. I had to work harder than others in order to prove that my promotions were justified. This is where I learned about systems and customer service, where the goal is to always provide the customer with the same great experience everytime they visit. That became my Big Why; provide the same memorable experience to each of my clients by using systems, people and technology.

When you have your first team member, your first follower, it's basically like when you have a child. You must lead by example. When I got my first assistant it felt a little strange because she was there waiting to take instruction from me and a lot of times I did not have any instructions to give! Since I didn't know what else to do, I told her to listen to me on the phone with my clients. I explained that this way, she would know how I work and when something came to mind, I could delegate it to her right away. That turned out to be the technique called shadowing; having a person follow you around and learn from what you are doing.

Just like with your child, you want your team members to be well-educated, so you have to provide the best training. If you are used to cutting corners you had better stop! You can no longer do this or your team members will follow suit and you'll end up with a mediocre business. You lead the way and shape your enterprise. Never assume anything. Never assume they know what they should be doing and what is not acceptable. Tell them exactly what you expect them to do and manage the outcome.

After you have trained your first assistant, an administrative person, who is now taking care of all non-licensed work, you will be freed up to complete more transactions. Personally, my goal was to be the best agent in Quebec for RE/MAX. My vision was that I should do more myself, as much as I could handle, working 7 days a week, 13-14 hours a day and delegate the rest. So for me, the next logical step was hiring a night time and weekend assistant. My broker's office had someone at night and on the weekend, so why not me? That would improve our customer service, and of course, free up some time for me to show homes and present offers. This decision turned out to create some challenges for me . . . I now had to find her work. She was there primarily to answer my calls, schedule my appointments and book appointments for other agents to show my listings. At first, it was a little boring for her because of the lack of work and poor organization of what I really wanted her to accomplish. But I found that after I took the time to explain my mission and vision, she became more engaged and was helpful in giving me her feedback on how to better service our clients. My goal became her goal. I was now leading 2 people while striving to reach my goal, and it felt great because my businesss was now starting to look like a real business.

Leading an administrative person and an agent is very similar, even though they have different personal goals. Administrative staff are usually looking for a consistent work week with the security of a paycheck every two weeks. Most agents are looking to make good money while also wanting to have some kind of freedom in their daily work schedule. Both types of team members need structure and want to have a plan. You must provide them with your Big Why.

Here is my Big Why, my mission and my vision.

- Being a leader in real estate by offering a highly professional service, by deploying our expertise, transparency and diligence, creating a memorable experience for our customers.
- Our vision is to be recognized for having the most efficient way of buying and selling real estate in Quebec, Canada, America, the world!
- We will do that with our unique team system, our Guaranteed Sales Program and our use of leading edge technology.
- We make buying and selling real estate more fun and rewarding.

I remember the first agent who joined my team. His name was Frank. I had advertised this position in all the area newspapers: Real estate agent needed, we supply the clients, no cold calling.

This a great ad Craig Proctor shared with us. Now the next step is crucial. When they meet with you, you have to show them how you are able to do this and why you choose to work this way. You need to be able to inspire confidence in your business, whether you're hiring your first or 10th agent.

I did a great job at the time of selling this position to Frank. I had no presentation or experience but I was able to convince him that he would make money, have time to enjoy it and that I was on a journey to become the best real estate team in Quebec. He joined me and I went on to expand my team. Now we have a complete system to hire agents, from the recruiting ads to the official presentation that compels the agent to join our team. Right down to the boarding process of getting started.

Early on in my team building process I decided to have a weekly meeting with my staff. At first, having a meeting with my 2 team members seemed a little unnecessary since we worked so closely, but it gave us the time to review our stats, our team procedures, our listings and to make sure I was providing enough feedback to my staff.

Attendance at my team meetings is mandatory. Early on, I decided to print a meeting schedule and all my team members can add a topic they wish to discuss. By having your staff participate, they will feel that they are building history with you and are part of something bigger than each individual.

As my team got bigger and my roles narrowed from being the technician to becoming the strategist, I slowly began spending less time with everyone. This is why during our Tuesday meetings I make sure I interact with all of my staff, to ensure that I am continuing to make them feel a part of my vision. Every week I put a minimum of 30 minutes into preparing for this meeting and I always name a moderator each week who makes sure that we stay on track.

My «Ordre du jour» goes like this.

1- 10:00am-10:05am — Welcome participants and opening words. (Performed by one of our agents, the Moderator) (he/she always opens with : refer us an agent and get 5% on his/her first 3 sales) We are always recruiting and want help from our agents.

2- 10:05am-10:15am — Word from our President. (That's me!)

3- 10:15am-10:25am — Challenge of the week. (I give advice and every agent can share their point of view)

4- 10:25am-10:35am — Success story. (Same thing here)

5- 10:35am-10:40am   - Networking events
6- 10:40am-10:55am   - You're looking for . . .(every agents needs to say
                          what their top 3 buyers are looking for. That way,
                          we can make a match with potential sellers)
7- 10:55am-11:00am   - Words from our sales manager. (Usually on the
                          team system and procedures)
8- 11:00am-11:10am   - Break
9- 11:10am-11:20am   - Team update with admin (We bring in our team
                          of admins, talk about upcoming team events, team
                          procedures, etc)
10- 11:20am-12:00pm   - Listing review. (We take a close look at our new
                          listings with pictures and a review of the others,
                          and talk about the upcoming listings).
11- 12 :00pm   - "Now go sell some houses!"

I also put the logo of our company on top of the meeting agenda. I brand
everything that we use. When I was with RE/MAX and was considering
leaving that company, an agent from another company told me: You agents
from RE/MAX think that they're the best and if you leave, your business
will drop. That's what successul agents with RE/MAX and other top
companies believe; that they are successul because of the company. This
makes them proud to work there. This is how I want my Team to feel. When
building your team, you will need to make sure that your staff believes in
you, and are proud to be a part of your team. Be proud of your team's image,
brand what you have built and are building.

When your team has enough leads to warrant hiring Inside Sales
Agents you will now be leading three different groups of people. The ISA's
job is to convert prospects to appointments and nurture them until they are
ready to meet with an Outside Sales agent. This is one of the most critical
and important jobs in your enterprise. So your role here as the leader is to
consistently let the ISA's know how important they are and how important
what they do is. In order to do that, guess what I have done? Yes, another
meeting. Every Wednesday afternoon, we meet for an hour to review their
numbers, see what is working and what's not. We also go over the numbers
to see how well the OSA's are doing converting those appointments to
contracts.

So as you can see, communication is extremely important for me in
leading my team.

When I first started to build my team, other agents would tell my
prospects that "If you go with Francois, you won't see him, he will send

other people that don't know anything about your home . . .". Also, early on, I had a case with a client that told me, "listen, I really like you, but 2 separate people from your team called me for the same info I gave you when you took the listing . . .". Since then, I've made it a point to have great communication with my team, the left hand MUST know what the right hand is doing.

Another thing that made me successful is the ability to keep people happy around me. Early on, I heard the quote : 'Your attitude determines your team's altitude'. So I worked on my attitude, making sure that I am always positive, always looking for solutions. When I am around my team, I am on the scene, so I have to be sharp, positive and professional so people will follow me in my journey.

The concept of on scene or behind the scene comes from Walt Disney. The concept is that when you are in Disney World, you will never see Mickey Mouse light up a cigarette, even if the actor in the costume does smoke, because this would destroy the magic. The actors, if on scene can never be themselves. You have to apply this concept in your business too. Once you step in the office, you are on scene, so you cannot be sad, mad, angry or give out negative energy. If you do you will have a hard time keeping good people. I often repeat this to my team, so that we have a great positive energy in the office, making it an attractive place to work.

A last note on your leadership as a real estate entrepreneur would be to work on yourself as your company grows. Your ability to support that growth will come with inner changes that will make you a better person and a better leader. Like Jim Rohn once said, "formal education will make you a living, self education will make you a fortune."

✦ ✦ ✦

Francois Mackay

In 1997, Francois's got his real estate licence at the age of 21 and teamed up with his mother, a successful real estate agent, top 10 for RE/MAX in Quebec since 1985. A few years earlier, François had been introduced to the business world, with networking companies such as Amway and Nikken and began to love personal development, reading books like *Unleash the Power Within* by Anthony Robbin and seeking out sales conferences. So it was with a great passion that when he started his real estate career, he wanted to become #1. After looking at what the top agents were doing, he soon realized that they all got their training at the same place . . . Craig Proctor's coaching. In 2002, he purchased Craig Proctor's Coaching Program and at the same time his mother retired. He was then working as a RE/MAX agent, with his secretary from his home garage and started to build his team. In 2004, for growth purposes, he changed his agency to go with Sutton Group and in 2010, after moving his office for a 2nd time into a 3200 square foot building, with 9 agents, started his own real estate company, Groupe Mackay, Real Estate Agency. Very much involved in his community, François is the Vice President of the Lachine Hospital foundation, has been president for many fund raising event such as the popular soup for people in need of food, the Parados, a shelter for abused women and an active supporter of sports programs for children. Groupe Mackay is now the #1 team in Quebec with over 460 transactions in 2014 and a group of 50 people with 35 agents providing superior service and delivering a memorable experience to their customers. François' vision is to be the first team to reach 1,000 sales in a year and this will be achieved by the end of 2016! (taking away $10,000 from Todd Walter's at the same time).

Chapter 22
The Team System at Work

by Francis Lavoie and
Audrey Bien-Aime

The Team System That Allows Us to Make A Sale Every 30 Hours

My wife Audrey and I firmly believe the only way to stand out from others is to know our competition and avoid making the same choices as them.

Always set the trail, never follow the path!

Why do like others when you can do things differently and probably better? My wife understood that this only happens when one is connected and surrounded by others. That is why she is the best recruiter of talent I know . . . She found me!

For a long time now we only select those agents who we believe are capable of working in an environment of total harmonious synergy. We understand that every customer who realizes his real estate dream is only made possible because of our team. We as a team reach our peak performance when **ALL** carry the trophy home. Teamwork is everything for us and that is why there is no letter **I** in the word **TEAM**!

Whenever we add a new member to our team we already know that it's a matter of time before he/she will become a star player, scoring many goals. We will do everything in our power to give the proper support, coaching and mentoring needed in order to achieve our common goal.

184

Working in synergy and synthesizing sectors.

We all know that one of the fears of an agent is to lose a prospect to a colleague. How can we look forward when we spend valuable time watching our back? Isn't the security that comes with being part of a team the element of persuasion used by most banners out there when trying to recruit agents - The strength of a team! Yet only a few have successfully achieved this ideal notion. This is because most agents work alone, thus goes the saying, "One can be lonely amidst the crowd".

Ultimately if agents are left to themselves they will end up performing all the tasks and assuming all the roles necessary in making a sale. Sourcing new prospects (Sellers/Buyers), market research, administration, marketing, accounting, visits and overseeing client's loyalty, just to name a few.

To score goals for the TEAM and not just for oneself

After years of confidence-based approaches, we were able to create the perfect team and score goals day after day. Picture a hockey or soccer team where each player knows his or her role to play. Each player knows instinctively what his/her teammate will do next or what position to be in to shoot & score. This is how you win the game! Therefore, Audrey and I decided to synthesize the sectors and allow some of our associates to be specialists in certain areas. By doing so, we have created a synergy between them. We have a marketing team that is efficient and open-minded. Together we are able to generate more business than anyone else.

We spend a lot of time studying the market and revising our plans. We are the 'Big Brothers' of our region. We

VOTRE PROPRIÉTÉ VENDUE
☑GARANTIE
OU JE L'ACHÈTE! *

GROUPE
LAVOIE

Francis Lavoie
Audrey Bien...

www.VendreMaintenant.net

450 635-0004
450 638-0000

RE/MAX
Platine F.L.

see everything! We spend many hours a week generating between 400 and 800 new leads per month using proprietary marketing systems where each element becomes an event. The lifeblood of our business is to generate prospects, without them, nothing would be possible.

Inside Sales: After generating all these leads, we need an effective follow up system. These members of our team are able to respond quickly to most of the needs that a potential or already registered client could have. Since most agents are either on the road, with a client, or perhaps even giving a comparative market analysis, our Inside Sales agents allow us to stay in close contact with our customers.

Those responsible for inside sales are well aware that buying a property is a process and not a rushed, one-time event. They therefore have a lot of patience. We no longer miss making follow up calls because they are always on the phones. One of our inside sales agents are always available to ensure that the customer will be called on time in order to book an appointment with either the buyer agent or listing agent.

We know the majority of buyers are not ready to make an offer or even visit a listing on their first call to the office. They first want to be informed about the market and how we do business. They need be assured that we will support them through the buying or selling process and that they can trust and respect us.

Our Buyer's agents are the best example of people who develop a humanistic approach and expertise in the field. A meeting with potential clients is not only to assess their needs but also to let them talk about their dream . . . and by doing so, we understand exactly what they are looking for. Since our buyer's agents are not spending time on all the other tasks an agent would normally do such as prospecting, administrative tasks, representing sellers, etc., they have more time to build a real relationship with the buyer and find the perfect home for them.

No customer should ever be overlooked. From the first meeting with a new client our buyers' agents will contact our listing agents. They can talk openly about the needs of their new customers and probably find that rare pearl among our listings or within our exclusive listings (sellers that have been met by our agents but were not ready to list their house on the market yet). They will also use their market intelligence to identify the good deals on the market, such as: foreclosures, out of the market properties, or even know of those in advance that are looking for a quick sale due to financial difficulties.

Since we have more than 200 buyers in waiting/listed in our database our prospective sellers understand that our team may already might have a buyer for their house before even meeting with us!

Our listing agents do hundreds of home estimates annually. Their skills allow them to estimate quite precisely the correct listing price for a property. They know the price it will sell for or and how long it will take to sell. They have the experience to offer sound advice on important aspects in order to maximize the asking price without lapsing into exaggeration.

When there's an offer to present, the seller can be sure that our agent will represent only the seller's best interests in the transaction since he is never in the position to represent the buyer in the transaction.

Our administrative associates: Not enough light in the living room? Rooms that seem too small? Someone needs to listen to the negative feedback from people who have visited a house. This information must absolutely be communicated to the seller and his agent.

Our administrative department manages the flow of information and frees our agents from the administrative expectations and necessary procedures. We all know that this aspect is often the most problematic for the agents as it takes time away from their clients. Things such as chasing missing documents, mortgage approval, inspection reports are all looked after by our administration department. This ongoing communication between our customers and our administrative support is the perfect way for the customer to feel really supported and get all their questions and concerns answered very quickly.

Coaching a team, not easy and yet so stimulating! "Groupe Lavoie" is a great team, where our first motivation lies in the happiness and pride of its collaborators. Our agents and associates are continuously training. We are always on the lookout for any new features that will give us the edge over our competition. As part of our Craig Proctor Coaching Program, and accompanied by our coach, Todd Walters, we travel North America to find new techniques to generate more business.

Audrey and I multiply efforts to make our group a true close knit family. Stability is important and we consider ourselves lucky to rely on our team to score so many goals. The fact that we complement each other is the reason we can take advantage of the talents of others while being able to develop our own strengths and natural abilities. We will stay the course with one of the largest and best teams in the world!

✦✦✦

Francis Lavoie and Audrey Bien-Aime

Both at the dawn of their thirties, Francis Lavoie and Audrey Bien-Aime have accumulated numerous successes early on in their respective lives. They are also parents of Thomas, a young boy who enjoys energy as extraordinary as that of his parents.

With over 10 years of experience and achievements in the real estate industry, Audrey and Francis are now owners and managers of the Groupe Lavoie (Lavoie Group) at RE/MAX Platinum F.L Agency.

Due to an exemplary growth, Lavoie Group ranks now among the best teams in sales for the RE/MAX banner. They are the number 1 team of all the South shore of Montreal. They also rank 4th in the entire Province of Quebec, among the 25 best in Canada, and top 60 worldwide. Francis and Audrey are a true model of what it means to have a healthy balance between family and success in business.

With the help of Craig Proctor coaching and their personal coach, Todd Walters, their reputation as well as their successes in real estate has allowed them to develop new, aggressive strategies whose effectiveness has been proven time and time again. All this in order to better respond and adjust quickly to the ever dynamic changing needs and concerns of sellers and buyers. They were interviewed by the *Canal Argent* (Money Channel) for their expertise on the South shore of Montreal and also by *Radio X*. Magazine *REM* (Real Estate Magazine), which is distributed to more than 70,000 brokers in the country, interviewed them to learn more about their success. They also gave an interview to the magazine *Above*, which is distributed to more than 96,000 Re/Max brokers worldwide.

At 29 years old, both are among the youngest Realtors in RE/MAX history to have been honored in 2012 by the Board of Directors, as well as the International Directors of RE/MAX. They have received the prestigious distinction of 'Lifetime Achievement Award'. This honor is awarded only to Realtors who have helped more than 1,000 families to buy or sell a property.

Francis & Audrey are also active investors in the real estate market owning many buildings both in Canada and the United States. Involved in their community, Francis and Audrey undertake a collection of funds each year for the benefit of Opération Enfants Soleil, while also financing local sports teams. They believe that their success and happiness allows them to give back to society and to ensure that everybody wins.

Chapter 23
Mission is Commission

by Justin Hoffmann and Todd Walters

If You Can Copy, You Can Succeed

I may have mentioned earlier in this book that the most difficult thing I do each day as a Millionaire Agent Maker Coach, working with Craig Proctor, is getting members to copy. I guess it's human nature for most agents to take something and tinker with it, spin it, or feel the need to monkey with it prior to just using it.

Over the last decade of coaching many of North America's top agents to help them create their Seven Figure Income Real Estate Businesses, I have been able to document commonalities among the upper-most successful members. You may want to grab a highlighter and mark what I'm about to reveal.

The commonalities among our most successful members, those making $1 Million to over $6 Million a year selling real estate, building Highly Profitable Real Estate Sales Teams are:

- *They are members of our Platinum Program*
- *They attend the live training events*
- *They hang out with OTHER Millionaire Agents*
- *They are very, very good copiers of what works*
- *They are fast implementers*

Moreover, what these agents do each day can be broken down into 5 categories:

1. *Cherry Pick Leads*
2. *Cherry Pick Appointments*
3. *Work ON Their Business (marketing, systems)*
4. *Recruit Team Members*
5. *Train Their Team*

Very few do this better than Justin Hoffman. Justin is a Millionaire Agent from the great state of Wisconsin. He is excellent at everything I have listed above. One of the extra characteristics that Justin possesses is that he is rarely satisfied with where his business is. There is much you can learn from the study of such individuals. I know it's common to study what they do and how they do things, but I would encourage you to look deeper and study how they think. **– Todd Walters**

✦ ✦ ✦

The Mission Is Commission

by Justin Hoffmann

I want you to imagine a systemized approach to selling Real Estate unlike anything you have ever been exposed to before. I want you to realize that the difference between average, good and great years are minor tweaks to your business.

I started selling Real Estate fulltime at the age of 21. I really had no idea what I was doing. I also want to point out that I have absolutely no College education whatsoever. Thank Goodness you don't need one to get a real estate license. In my first few years of selling houses I was what the industry refers to as a "Cold Call Cowboy". For my first 6 years in the business this worked well enough for me to earn a GCI of around $250k. It was a ceiling that I was unable to break through. By Summer of 2007, I was burnt out. I had a wife and 2 young kids that I rarely got to spend quality time with, and my business was stuck with a quarter million dollar annual gross earnings. It was at this point in my career that I knew something had to change.

I had heard about Craig Proctor, promoting himself as the guy who had it all figured out. He earned millions of dollars every year selling real estate and only worked 35-40 hours per week. Now to a young kid in his mid-20's, (that was completely burnt out of the business already) and working over 75 hours per week, this sounded too good to be true. But my curiosity got the best of me. I scratched up the money and headed to one of his conferences in July of 2007. I sat in the back of the Super Conference in absolute awe. **2,000 Realtors from all over North America listening to Craig break down his business step by step.** I can remember how overwhelmed I was and excited to get back to Milwaukee, WI and start crushing it. I also recall calling my father back in Wisconsin and talking a million miles an hour about how I was going to make a million dollars selling real estate, and only have to work 40 hours per week.

In the early months I struggled to get my systems in place and to re-learn the Real Estate business. But little by little, and with much help from Craig and his coaches like Todd Walters, I started to see big changes. **By 2009, I had already doubled my business to over $500k GCI. My business has grown by at least 25% every year since.** This year, we expect to close over 350 transactions and my GCI will have exploded to over $1.3M. My OSA's will all net over $100k with no expenses, and dozens of motivated leads are handed over to them every month. They are all very well-trained and excited to come to work every day.

Hands down, the most effective marketing program my team offers is the Guaranteed Sale Program (Your Home Sold Guaranteed or I'll Buy It*). Let me be clear in saying that I have absolutely no fear of this program whatsoever. I have literally made a couple million dollars using it. In the 5 years of offering the Guarantee I have only had to buy 2 houses, but have sold hundreds. The key component in this program is to never deviate from the spread, or the rules (conditions). To get a full understanding of the rules and the spread, it's best to be coached by Craig Proctor himself.

We market this program on everything from our email signature to our radio ads, our direct mail, sign riders, business cards, folders,

social media, and of course our websites. We have specific domain names to track where each lead comes from in our direct response marketing system. So this is how I know what works and what doesn't.

If you run an ad to attract prospects, but you cannot identify where the lead comes from, you are making a huge mistake. Every marketing system we use has consistent "trackable" results. This is key when deciding to cut one loose that loses money, or even beef one up that has more success. Just about every successful business has some form of a USP (Unique Selling Proposition). My successful Real Estate Team uses multiple USP's to differentiate ourselves from the competition and to attract more prospects.

My two favorite direct mail campaign postcards I use are "Your Home Sold Guaranteed or I'll Buy It" and "Your Home Sold in 89 days Guaranteed or I'll Pay You $5,000". We send this to every single FSBO and Expired listing in our marketplace. It comes in the mail to them as a 2-sided postcard with the USP on top, a call to action in the middle, our phone number, domain for the specific mailing, and of course, a deadline. In this case our domain for "Your Home Sold Guaranteed or I'll Buy it" is www.OurGuaranteedSalesProgram.com.

We have a specific landing page set up for all prospects to go to our website via that URL. We also have a deadline on all the post cards to create urgency and limited time to act within the mind of the prospects. The domain name for the other campaign is www.89DayHomeSale.com with its own unique landing page.

I send these postcards exactly one week apart to every single FSBO and Expired Listing. Our results from this simple postcard are awesome! We pull over 10 listings per month just from this one marketing program. 60% of the leads are from the USP "Your Home Sold Guaranteed or I'll Buy It".

We have an awesome listing presentation that we got from Todd Walters in the Platinum Program that gets over 90% of our prospects asking us where to sign. This whole direct mail system is completely duplicatable and costs me less than $2,000 per month to run including postage, payroll to send it, and the postcard itself. I do absolutely nothing to make this happen. I outsource to my printer, who also pulls the addresses, prints the labels and mails them for me. The ROI for this system alone is over $15 to $1. **If you are thinking of running this marketing program, make sure you have time set aside to list another 10 homes per month**. The key is being able to call or respond to all of these leads. You do not want to become a 'lead collector' and let these leads go with no follow up. Having a great database or CRM will allow a system to call these prospects back and book tons more appointments. Since I launched this marketing system in 2009, I have not cold called even one FSBO or Expired Seller. They pick up the phone and call me. Or, they will fill out the form on my landing page specifically designed for this campaign.

Realize this key component: I spend hours and hours and hours every single month networking and training with the absolute best Real Estate Agents in North America via the Craig Proctor Platinum Program. Success leaves clues. My mind now works differently than it did before Craig's Program. I can envision marketing programs that no one else is doing and make them a total success. One of my absolute favorite marketing campaigns for Short Sale Sellers, is the Wisconsin Short Sale Network I started.

Does this statement sound like your marketplace? Hundreds of under-qualified agents handling short sales, screwing them all up because they either don't know what the heck they're doing or they just don't have enough time to handle them correctly. My market was full of the above scene. Short Sales taking 6-9 months to end up falling apart and foreclosing anyway. I literally hated hearing the horror stories from my agents and other Realtors so I decided to become an absolute expert in the field. I accomplished this by literally flying all over the country. When I had it all figured it out I turned it into a step by step system. I also hired and trained a Short Sale Manager to handle all of my Short Sales from the time I list them all the way through closing. I literally worked like a mad scientist, flying all over the country to learn the absolute best practices for closing Short Sales. I completely reverse engineered the entire system by interviewing Asset Managers and Loss Mitigators from every major Bank in the USA. I took everything I had learned and systemized a manual so I could train someone else to do it for me. Now, I close 7-10 short sales every single month because of it. Where do all these leads come from you ask? They come from my competitors in my own market place! That's right! I am also marketing to my competitors too. Every single real estate agent in my marketplace gets quarterly emails, video emails and postcards. We market the URL www.WIShortSaleNetwork.com. Our message is simple. Stop wasting your time trying to list and close short sales. My team has the systems and manpower in place to get all of this done for you. All the agents have to do is log onto our website and fill out the page.

There is a section for the referral as well as who is referring it. The referring agent gets a referral form emailed to them offering them 20% of the commission earned upon successful closing. On auto pilot my team drafts a referral agreement and it emails the agent as well as shoots an intro email to the short sale sellers. We are listings tons of other agents' referrals from this awesome short sale system. Most of these listings are absolute lay downs too. The massive leverage from these kind of listings is also the amount of buyer leads they generate.

My OSA's have a field day converting these buyers that call in on our Short Sale listings. In addition to our For Sale Sign, we have what we refer to as Bandit Signs. These signs are placed next to the for sale sign with a message to the buyers. Simply stated, it is offering the prospect more heavily discounted distressed homes for sale.

This sign also has its own phone number and URL. We attract a ridiculous amount of stray buyers off of these bandit signs that we place next to our for sale signs on all of our Short Sale Listings and REO properties. In order to make over $1 million in GCI you must understand that Optimization is everything. We have the ability to massively leverage off of our popular listings to create more transactions. We do this by positioning and leveraging off of multiple signs to get traffic to our websites and make our phones ring off the hook with leads.

Truthfully, my Team has far more leads because of all of my systems than we really know what to do with. We are hiring and training all the time to create the absolute best Real Estate Team Wisconsin has ever seen. **It is really easy to recruit and retain agents when all they have to do is show up to work and they are showered with high quality and ready to act buyers and sellers.**

Ego plays a huge role in every successful person's life. If you ask anyone who knows me they will tell you that I have a huge ego. I would agree with that, and also tell you that a big ego can be as much a positive as a negative in business.

Image ads that I used to use and that my competitors still use, beef egos and bust bank accounts. These types of ads don't work. Nobody cares about you as the agent. All they care about is what is in it for them. They all tune into the same radio station called WIFM Radio (What's In It For Me). I am able to get the best of both worlds with my awesome radio ads.

I used to only get my ego boosted when I ran radio ads. All they did was make me feel good for about $3,000 per month. They hardly generated any leads and in the end they lost me lots of money. **Thanks to hanging out with Millionaire and Multi-Millionaire Agents, now I know better and my ads are different**. I use a celebrity talk show radio host that endorses me. Obviously, it takes more than a celebrity endorsement to make an ad successful. I also have the celebrity bragging about my Unique Selling Propositions. Including, but not limited to, Our Guaranteed Sale

Program, and Fire me at any time option. These ads are strategically run at key times to maximize the amount of listeners in the audience. This gives me the ego boost as well as makes me a ton of money. I have The Sean Hannity as my endorsement. It costs far less than you think and the ROI is huge. The right endorsement combined with right message, run at the right time, equates to big ROI.

This celebrity endorsement also makes me a mini celebrity in my market area. My competitors hate me for it and that is an awesome feeling. There is nothing better than legally stealing your competitors' business with awesome marketing. Radio ads will instantly change your life and business for the better. You are able to reach thousands of people every day with a perfect message to market match spoken by a gigantic celebrity. All of my radio ads can be heard on YouTube, key word 'Team Hoffmann'.

These are only 3 of my favorite money making marketing campaigns. Bottom line is, even if I did nothing else to promote or market my Team, I could make a decent living off of the three mentioned above. One of the key components in running a successful Real Estate Team is hiring the right people. Turnover is part of the business but you must have a system for hiring as well. You can never lower your standards because of the people around you. Raise the bar higher and higher every year and expect to achieve your goals. But let's be clear here. Just because you gross over $1 million in commission doesn't make you a millionaire. The only thing that matters is your bottom line profit.

If you are spending money on something, you must demand a positive return on the investment. That is why we track everything to determine whether or not it is worth the money it costs. As soon as it proves to be unsuccessful, we kill it immediately. You also must keep very good books. I strongly recommend a bookkeeper or accountant to give you monthly profit and loss statements. I have one statement made up for each marketing campaign that I spend money on. The only way to make really good business decisions is to have really good book keeping.

I also have a wealth building system that I want to share with you. All of my Team members are exposed to more than just how to make money via a commission check. I have turned to automation to build actual wealth. 15% of every gross commission check I earn is auto deposited into a separate interest bearing checking account. This account is only used for buying other tangible long term investments.

For example, I buy stocks, Real Estate, and contribute funds to my retirement accounts. I have been buying and renting houses since I got into the business at 21 years old. I also run a property management company.

As I built my business over the years, I always wanted to be diversified in my revenue streams. I like to refer to them more as "revenue rivers". We earn income from 5 major different pillars. Retail Sellers and Buyers, Short Sale Sellers and Buyers, REO Listings and Sales, Rental Income, and Property Management Income.

All of my rental property has to cash flow on a 15 year mortgage. My mortgage payments are set to be auto debited from my accounts every month. They are all on 15 year notes and I add 10% to the principle every month, automatically. **With this system I will be able to afford to never sell another house again, and have completely replaced my commission income in less than 10 years at the age of 40. This is real wealth.** The key is buying cash producing assets that appreciate over time while paying down the principle. This is how wealth is built in anything. I also have committed to living within my means. I can't tell you how many high commission, low net worth Realtors I have met over the years that are flat broke. It bothers me to no end that many Realtors make poor financial decisions and have no clue how to grow their nest egg to retire one day.

Automation is the key component to building wealth. You should set even just your own home mortgage to automatically come out of your account every month and add 10% to the principle. Pay off the debt. Stay away from brand new cars that do nothing more than depreciate quicker than anything else on earth that you can purchase.

Please understand that as self-employed people we also need to put aside enough money every month to pay Uncle Sam. This money is separately deducted from your account and put into your 'Tax Account". Look, nobody likes paying taxes, but do not get yourself in trouble with the IRS. They will make your life absolutely miserable and they make horrible business partners. Get with a well-versed CPA and discover tax deferment strategies. There are still many options to bury income and build wealth, all while deferring taxes or straight up writing it off.

Now get out there and change your business with a few easy-to-duplicate marketing systems that will blow your sales up. These are all very profitable and tested for success. Google has become a very powerful way to find out how to get in touch with the right people to help put these systems together. Whether you need training from Craig Proctor, want to run radio ads with Matt Wagner, or need a printer to run your direct mail campaign with Exclusively Cards Inc., remember to pay yourself first with an auto debit into a long-term savings account.

I don't only run the #1 Real Estate Team in Wisconsin. I also run the "Team to be at" in Wisconsin. I draw motivated people who want not only to become successful real estate agents, but who also want to learn direct from me on how to become a millionaire. I have all the leads, training, and systems to sell dozens of homes every month, while automatically gaining long term wealth that anybody can duplicate.

Justin Hoffmann

Justin Hoffmann has turning the heads of Real Estate Professionals in the state of Wisconsin since he started selling homes at the age of 21. Innovative, aggressive and a natural born leader are the qualities that Justin possesses that have catapulted his real estate career.

Team Hoffmann, the Real estate team that Justin runs, has sold over 1,700 homes in the past 13 years. He has been recognized as the #1 RE/MAX Agent in all of WI and has earned the highest level awards from the company possible including Chairman's Club and the Lifetime Achievement award. Justin is also an avid real estate investor and runs a successful property management company.

Justin is a member of the elite Titanium Group run by Todd Walters and Craig Proctor, consisting of agents in the top 0.5% of North America. Past awards include being recognized by the Craig Proctor Coaching staff for his team's exceptional gains as recipient of the 2013 Quantum Leap Award.

Since 2013, Justin has worked for Craig Proctor, training real estate agents around North America to Quantum Leap their businesses. Justin is a frequent public speaker on real estate topics such as marketing, negotiations, seller pricing strategy, selling homes as-is and finding off-market properties for buyers.

Building his team to run like a systemized machine has allowed him to also spend time doing things he enjoys. Justin is a Youth Football Coach and has coached National Championship winning teams for the last several years. Justin also enjoys golfing and earning his black belt in taekwondo. Justin has been married to his wife Michelle for 13 years and they have 2 children, Dominic age 14, and Alyssa age 12.

Chapter 24
Not the End

by Todd Walters

You now have The Book with details and proof that a highly profitable sales team is not only a trend, but the pathway to a better real estate business for you and your clients. But this book is only one 'tool' in a whole SYSTEM of smart, sophisticated, proven, profitable marketing and success systems we would like to invite you to use as your own . . . and we would like you to check out these systems, and judge for yourself whether this book should end our relationship or begin it.

As the owner of this book you are entitled to a free ***Real Estate Business Coaching Consultation*** as well as Free Training with Craig Proctor Real Estate Coaching. This free training and consultation includes real life examples of The Quantum Leap System and how you can use this POWER BUSINESS BUILDING SYSTEM to dramatically increase your business and lifestyle.

To claim your free business building training and coaching consult visit **www.YourRealEstateSuccessTeam.com**

*offer subject to change.

Lightning Source UK Ltd.
Milton Keynes UK
UKOW03f0338260517
302026UK00001B/93/P